Annual Survey

Business

Andrew Gillespie

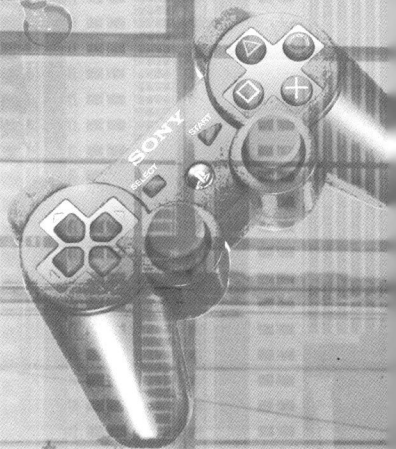

Philip Allan Updates
Market Place
Deddington
OX15 0SE

Orders
Bookpoint Ltd, 130 Milton Park, Abingdon, Oxfordshire, OX14 4SB
tel: 01235 827720
fax: 01235 400454
e-mail: uk.orders@bookpoint.co.uk
Lines are open 9.00 a.m.–5.00 p.m., Monday to Saturday, with a 24-hour
message answering service. You can also order through the Philip Allan
Updates website: www.philipallan.co.uk

© Philip Allan Updates 2007

ISBN 978-1-84489-628-8

Printed by Raithby, Lawrence & Co Ltd, Leicester

Environmental information
The paper on which this title is printed is sourced from managed, sustainable
forests.

P00881

Contents

Introduction

This *Business Annual Survey* aims to give you an insight into some of the key business stories of 2006. It will help to broaden your understanding of the main issues and provide a background to your analysis of other business cases. The survey is organised in a way that allows you to dip into different stories to find out more about a particular aspect of business. It is packed with relevant stories that will widen and deepen your awareness of the business world, whether you are studying at AS or A2. It should prove invaluable for developing the ability to apply your business understanding and for comparing the actions of firms and markets. As well as being an enjoyable read, the survey will help you to build the skills needed for exam success.

The book is divided into sections that focus on important business issues, so that you can find out about a particular area of interest (e.g. the part of the specification that you happen to be studying). Remember that, although this survey will help you to look back at 2006, you should also be reading newspapers and listening to business programmes as much as possible in order to keep up to date with developments. In some cases, you will be able to see how stories that emerged in 2006 have developed.

Each business story ends with a question that highlights the key issues raised. Answer notes are given on pages 67–74, but you should try to work out your own responses first. Finally, in the back of the book, there is a quiz containing 50 questions that tests how much you have learned about 2006.

This is the first *Business Annual Survey*, so any feedback would be appreciated. You can send your comments by e-mail to wattgill@aol.com.

Andrew Gillespie

Chapter 1

The biggest, fastest and best

About this chapter

This section provides an overview of some of the biggest and best companies in the UK in 2006, starting with private firms. Public limited companies are often the most high-profile organisations, but the significance of private limited companies should not be ignored. Most companies are privately owned and they contribute enormously to the economy. The fastest-growing company in the UK last year was GHD, which produces hairstyling irons. The largest private company was the gambling firm Gala Coral.

There are many advantages to being a private firm, such as less pressure from outside investors. Many UK managers in public limited companies complain that investors pressurise them for short-term rewards, which prevents them from investing sufficiently for the long term. This is one reason for the growth of private equity firms, which buy public companies and turn them private, so that they can run them how they want. Having made these companies more successful, they float them at a higher value than they were bought for.

Of course, there is more to business than being the biggest or the fastest-growing. Some firms are also interested in their effect on the environment and in how they treat their employees or other stakeholder groups. W. L. Gore was voted best UK employer of 2006 because it generates an environment in which employees want to work. This may be due in part to the rewards that the company offers, but, more importantly, it is an organisation in which people are valued and looked after. Marks and Spencer plc also did well in 2006, winning an award from Business in the Community for its dealings with suppliers and its focus on Fairtrade. In contrast, E.ON did less well and was named, along with other energy companies, as 'polluter of the year'.

Not all companies are based solely in the UK, so this chapter includes a selection of the most attractive countries in which to do business. These countries can appeal to firms because of their good infrastructure, lack of corruption or low taxes. However, operating in other countries can be difficult because of local regulations or lack of support services.

Also in this chapter is a list of the ten biggest global companies. These huge organisations have market values of billions of dollars and exercise incredible power worldwide. Compare these businesses with Built from Scratch Designs Ltd — a new company that is just beginning to expand and has won the Shell LiveWire Young Entrepreneur Award in 2006.

The UK's fastest-growing private company

According to the Oxford-based research company Fast Track, the fastest-growing private company in the UK in 2006 was GHD. The firm sells over 2 million ceramic styling irons a year to hair salons and direct to consumers. Its average sales growth has been over 360% per year since it was set up in 2001. Annual sales are now worth over £40 million. Celebrities such as Madonna, Gwyneth Paltrow, Jennifer Aniston and Victoria Beckham have all used the firm's products.

The business was started with just £15,000, and initially the hair tongs were sold only through upmarket West End hair salons rather than in high-street stores. GHD is now launching a range of 30 haircare products under the brand name nu:u. One of the company's founders, Martin Penny, signed a deal in 2006 with Lloyds Development Capital to buy out the share of co-founders Gary Douglas and Robert Powls for £55 million, valuing the whole business at £120 million.

Q1.1   What are the main problems that GHD might face in the future?

Growth strategy of the year

The winner of the National Business Award for Growth in 2006 was Speedy Hire, a provider of equipment hire services to UK contractors and builders, in industry and the public sector. The company operates from 300 depots around the UK, focusing mainly on tool hire, but it has other businesses that specialise in portable accommodation, surveying and power-generation equipment.

The construction industry has experienced annual growth of around only 3% in recent years, but Speedy Hire has grown at an average of 23% a year. The company's vision is 'to be number one in everything it does', from health and safety to quality of delivery. It spends heavily on updating equipment and motivates staff through large bonuses. Speedy Hire's ethos is illustrated in the company's vision statement: 'Speedy endeavours to employ the best, devolve responsibility where possible, encourage and support their development, and reward well for success and loyalty…Speedy works hard to maintain its "can-do" culture.'

Q1.2   What is meant by a 'can-do' culture? How can such a culture be developed in a business?

The UK's biggest private companies

Each year, the Oxford-based research company Fast Track produces a league table of the largest private businesses in the UK. Top of the table in 2006 was Gala Coral, a company formed in October 2005 when the Gala group acquired

Coral Eurobet for £2.2 billion. Gala runs bingo clubs and casinos, whereas Coral Eurobet focuses on high-street, telephone and online betting. The business employs over 17,000 people and has a turnover of over £74 million.

At number two in the league table was the John Lewis Partnership, which has 27 John Lewis stores, 179 Waitrose stores and a 33% share in the online delivery business Ocado. Sales for the John Lewis Partnership in the year to January 2006 were £5,149 million. In 2006, the business announced the appointment of its first non-executive directors — people who sit on the board of directors but do not have a full-time role in the company. Non-executive directors can offer less biased views of decisions and can bring more experience of other industries and firms.

The third largest private business was Somerfield, the supermarket chain, which changed from public to private company in December 2005. It used to include the KwikSave chain, but these stores have now been rebranded as Somerfield. Sales at Somerfield in 2005 were worth over £4,500 million.

Other well-known private companies in the UK include:
- AA (motor services)
- Arcadia (fashion retailer including Dorothy Perkins, Burton and TopShop)
- BHS (department store)
- C&J Clark (Clarks shoes)
- JCB (construction equipment)
- Iceland (frozen-food retailer)
- Kwik-Fit (car repair)
- Odeon and UCI Cinemas (cinema operator)
- Peacock Group (retailer)
- River Island (fashion retailer)
- Thresher (off-licence)
- Trailfinders (travel agency)
- Virgin Atlantic (airline and tour operator)
- Welcome Break (motorway services)

Q1.3 Why might firms want to remain private rather than become public limited companies?

The UK's fastest-growing technology companies

The fastest-growing technology company in 2006 was Gamesys, according to the *Sunday Times* Tech Track league table. Gamesys is an online gambling business that runs a website specialising in bingo, instant-win games and casino tables. Since its creation in 2001, the website has acquired 900,000 subscribers, over half of whom are women. The company operates gaming sites along with well-known consumer brands such as Orange and GMTV. Annual sales have grown over 300% in recent years, rising from £587,000 in 2003 to £9 million in 2005. In 2006 the company processed 150 million cash bets.

Q1.4   Why do you think that Gamesys has grown so fast?

The UK's best employer

According to the 2006 survey by the *Sunday Times*, the best employer in the UK was W. L. Gore Associates (a company that was set up by Bill and Vieve Gore in 1958). This was the third time that the company had won the award. The company's products (e.g. Gore-tex waterproof fabric) are used all over the world and can be found in such varied items as computer cables, guitar strings, spacesuits and skiwear. The firm has two bases in the UK; both are known to have a high level of creativity and employee commitment.

The scores given by the company's staff in the survey are listed in Table 1.1.

Criterion	Employees who agree (%)
Belief in the values of the organisation	93%
Pride in working for Gore	93%
Being able to make a difference	92%
Loving their jobs	90%

Table 1.1

Employees at W. L. Gore may have such high levels of satisfaction because the business lacks layers of hierarchy. All members of staff are called 'associates' and they help to decide their colleagues' pay. John Kennedy, the company's UK representative, says: 'We believe in the individual. If you treat them right they will do good things.'

To maintain such a positive environment, new recruits at W. L. Gore are chosen carefully. Potential employees are interviewed for up to 8 hours over 3 days. These efforts seem to pay off: more than half the staff members have worked at the company for at least 10 years and 75% say that they have their dream job.

W. L. Gore achieved UK sales of £105.9 million in 2006 and made profits of £14.6 million. In addition to spending £48,000 on social events, the company offers its associates a final-salary pension scheme, 26 weeks' fully paid maternity leave and private healthcare. There is also a share-option scheme and profit-related pay. Flexible working opportunities enable staff members to balance their responsibilities at home and at work.

Q1.5   How might W. L. Gore benefit from having a highly satisfied workforce?

Business in the Community

Business in the Community (BITC) is an organisation that measures and reports on socially responsible business practice. It has 131 member organisations, representing 4.2 million employees and a total turnover of £688.6 billion. In its 2006 survey, BITC found that:
- 57% of its organisations were focusing on diversity (i.e. having a diverse workforce), employee welfare and development
- 69% had energy-efficiency programmes
- 80% reported on key social and environmental issues

In 2006, Marks and Spencer plc was named as Business in the Community's Company of the Year for achievements that included:
- becoming the first high-street retailer to sell Fairtrade cotton clothing
- guaranteeing UK dairy farmers fixed prices
- converting all its sandwich packaging to cardboard sourced from sustainable forests

This was the second time that Marks and Spencer had been named Company of the Year by BITC (the first time was in 2004).

Q1.6   How can organisations benefit from working with their stakeholders and local communities?

The UK's biggest polluters

According to a study by the *Guardian* newspaper, five UK companies produce more carbon dioxide pollution together than all the vehicle drivers in the UK. The top five UK business polluters — E.ON UK, RWE npower, Drax, Corus and EDF — emitted over 100 million tonnes of carbon dioxide in 2006. Typically, the UK's car drivers produce just over 90 million tonnes.

E.ON UK, the electricity generator that owns Powergen, was identified as the company that generates the greatest amount of carbon dioxide: 26.4 million tonnes in 2006, which, according to the *Guardian*, exceeds the quantity produced by the whole of Croatia.

Q1.7   To what extent should firms seek to reduce their output of harmful emissions?

Most attractive countries

Table 1.2 lists some of the most attractive countries in which to do business (scored out of 10).

Ranking	Country	Score
1	Denmark	8.82
2	Finland	8.70
3	Canada	8.68
7	UK	8.64
8	USA	8.63
14	Germany	8.33
17	France	8.16
28	Japan	7.41
38	Italy	7.07
50	China	6.39
58	India	6.15
62	Russia	6.02

Source: Economist Intelligence Unit

Table 1.2

The business environment in each country is ranked on the basis of 90 factors, such as market opportunities, tax, financing opportunities, labour market and infrastructure.

Q1.8   What makes the UK an attractive country in which to do business?

The top ten global companies

The top ten global companies of 2006 are listed in Table 1.3.

Ranking	Company	Country	Products/type of business	Market value ($m)	Turnover ($m)
1	Exxon Mobil	USA	Oil and gas	371,631	358,955
2	General Electric	USA	General industrials	362,526	148,019
3	Microsoft	USA	Software and computer services	281,170	39,788
4	Citigroup	USA	Bank	238,935	n/a
5	BP	UK	Oil and gas	233,259	249,465
6	Bank of America	USA	Bank	211,706	n/a
7	Royal Dutch Shell	UK	Oil and gas	211,279	306,731
8	Wal-Mart stores	USA	Retailer	196,859	312,427
9	Toyota Motor	Japan	Automobiles	196,730	157,997
10	Gazprom	Russia	Oil and gas	196,338	35,485

Source: Economist Intelligence Unit

Table 1.3 Top ten global companies of 2006 according to market value

Q1.9 Why are so many of the largest companies in the oil and gas or banking industries? Why are so many of them American?

Young Entrepreneur of the Year

The LiveWire scheme run by oil company Shell aims to 'nurture and value business innovation'. The 2006 winner was Built from Scratch Designs Ltd, which describes itself as concept makers, product designers, innovators and functional artists. The company's most successful product to date is the Cyclepod, a new-age bicycle storage system. According to the company's website:

> Cyclepods has created a form of cycle storage, shelter and parking like nothing out there at the moment. It not only looks modern, novel and exciting but it also maximises space allowing eight bikes to be stored in a 2-metre diameter…The new product is more secure than any other form of cycle parking as cyclists can lock both the frame of the bike and the wheel to the unit using almost any type of lock.

With the growth in the number of cyclists in the UK, combined with fears concerning the security of bikes, this product has high potential for sales.

Q1.10 Why has the number of cyclists in the UK increased?

Chapter 2

People in business

About this chapter

Often in business we talk about a firm or a business deciding to do something. Of course, firms and businesses do not decide anything — people do. A company may exist in law as a separate legal entity, but the actual decisions are made by the owners or the employees. People are ultimately responsible for the success or failure of a business. This explains why newspapers carry stories about business individuals and examine their careers as well as reporting on the progress of their companies.

In 2006, a well-known business figure called Ken Lay died. Lay worked for Enron, the US company that went into bankruptcy in 2001 when it was discovered that its reported profits did not exist. Another Enron executive, Jeffrey Skilling, was sentenced to 24 years in prison.

Sir Ken Morrison also featured quite regularly in the news. He had led the Wm Morrison supermarket group to great success over many years, but his judgement was called into question following the purchase of Safeway plc. The takeover by Morrisons of a much bigger company led to major culture clashes and a disappointing performance by the combined business. Analysts felt that Sir Ken's hands-on management style was not suited to the much bigger organisation. As the company struggled to deliver the promised results, questions were raised about Sir Ken's role, in particular as chairman of the board of directors and chief executive. This forced him to appoint new directors, and eventually he agreed to stand down.

Another figure who refused to leave the front pages was Gerald Ratner. After an embarrassing speech in 1991 in which he criticised his own company, Ratner was forced to resign as chief executive. Years later he returned to try to buy the business. Unfortunately for him, the financial situation of one of his businesses was questioned by the auditors and this hindered Ratner's ability to borrow money.

Some of the people in the business media in 2006 are new-comers who may have great careers ahead of them. Among them is Oliver Bridge, who set up the footwear company Bigger Feet. Having big feet himself he identified a niche in the market — a good example of matching personal skills and interests to market needs.

The final part of this chapter profiles Maarten van den Bergh, the man whom the *Sunday Times* named as the most powerful person in UK business because of his connections.

The death of Ken Lay

In May 2006, Ken Lay, a senior manager at Enron, died while awaiting trial for six counts of conspiracy and fraud. Some analysts believe that he was responsible for the failure of Enron, but Lay had always claimed that he knew nothing about the fraud. Set up in 1985, Enron grew in just 17 years from being a small business to the USA's seventh largest company, employing 21,000 staff in over 40 countries. However, this amazing growth proved to be extremely misleading and turned out to be based on accounting fraud and misrepresentation. Employees at Enron falsely reported its profits and the company was closed in December 2002. Accounting firm Arthur Andersen (Enron's auditors) was also involved in the crisis — the business collapsed after being found guilty of deliberately destroying evidence of its relationship with Enron.

In October 2006, another former Enron executive, Jeffrey Skilling, was sentenced to 24 years in prison for his role in the company's collapse. In May, he was found guilty of 19 counts, including fraud, conspiracy and insider trading.

The fall of Enron was dramatic. In just 3 months it went from being a company with a value of $62 billion to being bankrupt (Figure 2.1).

Figure 2.1 Fluctuations in Enron's share price

Q2.1 Do you think that shareholders can ever be safe from fraud such as in the Enron case?

Teenage tycoon

The BBC's *Money Programme* featured a number of 'teenage tycoons' in 2006, including Oliver Bridge, who set up the shoe company Bigger Feet at the age of 15. When he was a teenager, Bridge could not find size 13 shoes and realised that there must be a gap in the market for people who need big shoes, so he started Bigger Feet Ltd in September 2004, with co-founder Paul Wilkinson. The company has received media coverage in the *Financial Times*, *Daily Mail*, *Independent on Sunday* and *Director* magazine, as well as on CNN, ITV1's *Five O'Clock Show* and BBC1's *Breakfast News*. Bridge also won the Enterprising Young Brit Award, which is a joint venture between Enterprise Insight, Lloyds TSB and the *Daily Mail*. Bigger Feet is a web-based company (www.biggerfeet.co.uk), which helps to keep costs down and prices low. Bridge will take his A-levels in 2007 and hopes to go to Oxford University and become a lawyer.

Q2.2 Do you think that the company Bigger Feet is likely to succeed in the long term?

Ken Morrison and Wm Morrison

In 2006, Sir Ken Morrison, the executive chairman of Wm Morrison, agreed to step down from the day-to-day operations of the business that he had run for nearly 50 years. Changes at the company involved a separation of the role of chairman and chief executive. Sir Ken continues as chairman of the board but is no longer the chief executive.

The restructuring took place after several difficult years for the company, following its £3.35 billion acquisition of Safeway. In 2006, Morrisons announced a loss for the first time in its 107-year history, which was caused by problems in integrating Safeway. Before the acquisition in 2002, Morrisons made a pre-tax profit of £279 million. Sir Ken has told shareholders that he will step down as chairman at the beginning of 2008 and become life president of the company.

Q2.3 What are the possible benefits of separating the roles of chairman of the board and chief executive?

Ratner's back

Gerald Ratner was once the leading figure in the retail jewellery market until he criticised one of his own products in an after-dinner speech in 1991. Although his career suffered, Ratner returned in 2006 to seek backing for a £200-million bid to buy the UK arm of Signet (which includes H. Samuel and Ernest Jones).

This was the business that he founded in the 1980s and led until 1991 (when he made his disastrous speech). However, Ratner's plans were interrupted when the latest accounts of a business linked to him included a warning about its financial strength. The business is called SB&T and supplies jewellery to television shopping firms and provides services to online retailer Geraldonline.com. The auditor said that 'conditions indicate the existence of a material uncertainty, which may cast doubt about the company's ability to continue as a going concern'. Ratner is a director of the company and a major shareholder.

Q2.4   Auditors are paid by the company whose accounts they inspect. Why might this cause problems?

Most powerful person in UK business

Each year the *Sunday Times* produces a list of the 100 most powerful people in UK business. Top of the list in 2006 was Maarten van den Bergh, whose roles include:
- non-executive chairman of Lloyds TSB (banking and finance; earnings £454,000)
- non-executive director of:
  - Royal Dutch Shell (natural resources; earnings £63,630)
  - BT Group (telecoms; earnings £55,000)
  - British Airways (transport; earnings £38,000)

Van den Bergh spent most of his career in the oil industry. He worked for Shell for 32 years and became the group's managing director in 1992. He stepped down in 2000, but rejoined as a non-executive director in 2005. In 2001, he became chairman of Lloyds TSB, having served as deputy chairman since 2000. It was in that year that van den Bergh took up his role at BT. He was appointed to the British Airways board as a non-executive director in 2002.

Q2.5   What is a 'non-executive director'? What are the benefits of having non-executive directors on the board?

Chapter 3

Say goodbye

About this chapter

There were many new start-up companies in 2006 (as in any year), but many brands and products also came to an end. The product life cycle highlights how products often go through a growth stage before maturing and finally entering into decline. How long this process takes depends on the type of product. For example, a particular model of computer can have a life span of months, whereas cigarette brands may last for many years. The 'death' of a product may be caused by technological developments, new competitors in the market or a change in trends away from particular goods or lifestyles. For example, as the UK population ages, there has been a boom in goods and services such as care homes and medicines but a decline in demand for skateboards.

Among the high-profile product deaths of 2006 were the music television programme *Top of the Pops* and the teenage magazine *Smash Hits*. The withdrawal of these products resulted from a change in consumer tastes and increased competition from other media, especially the internet. Meanwhile, model manufacturer Airfix suffered as teenagers chose to play computer games instead of buying its kits. The company has, however, now been rescued by the model train manufacturer, Hornby.

Aston Martin, the luxury car brand, has not disappeared, but it is for sale. Its owner, Ford, needs to focus on its core business and raise finance. The skills and assets necessary to promote and develop the Aston Martin brand may not sit comfortably with Ford, which is a mass-market producer.

Another product that struggled to make an impact in the UK was the Segway scooter. It was expected to revolutionise transport when first launched in 2002, but it failed to capture the public's imagination. The Segway was dealt a major blow by UK legislation that restricted its use.

The stories in this chapter show that even long-established brands can disappear eventually. No business or product is safe forever. Managers need to be aware of future opportunities and threats (whether external change or internal problems) and plan accordingly.

Top of the Pops

After 42 years, the BBC's television programme *Top of the Pops* was shown for the last time on 30 July 2006. 'The time has come to bring the show to its natural conclusion,' said the BBC's director of television, Jana Bennett. The programme could no longer compete with 24-hour music channels. *Top of the*

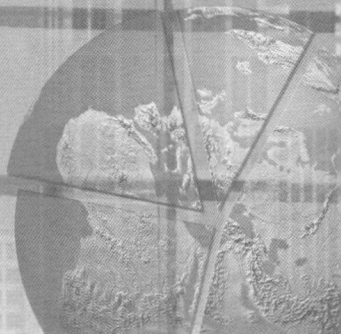

Pops was first broadcast in 1964 from a converted church in Manchester and was presented by Radio 1 DJ Jimmy Savile. In its prime in the 1970s, the show had audiences of 15 million, but by 2002 the viewing figures had dropped to just 3 million. The programme was relaunched in 2003 with former presenter Andi Peters in charge, but it failed to attract new viewers and was moved from BBC1 to BBC2 in 2004.

Q3.1 Why do you think that *Top of the Pops* was taken off the air?

Smash Hits

Smash Hits, a pop magazine that had been published for almost 30 years, was finally withdrawn in 2006. The magazine closed because of competition from new media and a decline in advertising from food and soft drinks companies. Its readership had been getting younger, as older readers switched to the internet. Circulation fell from 1 million in 1989 to just 120,000 in 2005. Other titles such as *CD:UK*, *Popworld* and *Live and Kicking* were also closed down.

Smash Hits was launched in 1978 and was a massive success, but its traditional target consumers (11–14-year-old girls) now have more choice of what to read and where to get information. More of the target consumers' pocket money is also being spent on mobile phones rather than magazines. The average age of *Smash Hits* readers had fallen to under 10 years old.

Another problem that *Smash Hits* faced was that most of its advertising was bought by the food and drink industries. Firms in these sectors are now concerned about being seen to target young children, so they are withdrawing their adverts, thus removing a major source of revenue for magazines such as *Smash Hits*. However, the *Smash Hits* brand will continue as a website, a television channel with 5.3 million viewers per month and a radio station with a weekly audience of 788,000.

Q3.2 Why are some firms worried about directing their advertising campaigns at children?

Airfix

Airfix was first established in 1939, producing plastic aeroplane kits that buyers assembled and painted. Its range developed to include planes, ships and tanks from the Second World War, as well as motorbikes, figures, trains, spaceships and science-fiction and film characters. It is owned by Hull-based firm Humbrol, which called in the receivers in 2006, leaving the future of Airfix in some doubt. Airfix first went into receivership in 1981, but it was later bought by Humbrol in 1986. Humbrol also produces Plasticine, Supercast and Young Scientist.

In November 2006, Hornby, the model train manufacturer, bought Airfix for £2.6 million. The Chief Executive claimed there was a good strategic fit and that both were iconic brands. Hornby intends to move the distribution, sales and marketing of Airfix to its own site in Kent, and outsource the manufacturing and assembly division.

Q3.3 Why do you think Airfix ran into trouble?

Aston Martin

The car company Aston Martin (forever associated with James Bond) was put up for sale in 2006 by its owner, Ford. It is one of three luxury marques owned by the company: the other two are Jaguar and Landrover, and together they form the Premier Automotive Group. A Ford spokesman said, 'As part of our ongoing strategic review we have determined that Aston Martin may be an attractive opportunity to raise capital and generate value.' The first Aston Martin was produced in 1914. The company was later bought by a tractor manufacturer called David Brown, under whose control many of the famous models were developed, such as the original DB5. However, the company went into receivership in 1974. In 1987, Ford bought 75% of the company and in 1993 bought the remaining 25%. Ford brought out the DB7 and expanded production to thousands rather than hundreds.

Q3.4 What factors are likely to determine the price that Ford will get for Aston Martin? Why sell the company now?

The Segway

In 2006, the UK government invoked the 1835 Highway Act to ban Segway scooters from pavements, and EU rules to keep them off the roads. The Segway is a self-balancing scooter that was launched in 2001 and was expected to change completely the way we travel in cities. France, Spain and most US states permit its use on pavements; Austria and the Netherlands allow it to be used on cycle paths, and in Italy it can be ridden on both. A spokesman for BAe systems that helped develop the gyroscopes in the Segway criticised the UK government as 'seem[ing] reluctant to accept new technology'.

Q3.5 How could Segway try to change the UK government's decision?

Chapter 4

Marketing

About this chapter

The marketing process involves identifying and even anticipating customer needs and then developing appropriate product and price, promotion and distribution strategies to meet these needs, while also satisfying the organisation's requirements. Over time, customers' needs change, which means that businesses must monitor their external environment and respond accordingly — for example, the move by supermarkets into organic foods. Another example is the launch of Coke Zero, which aimed to broaden Coca-Cola's portfolio and meet consumer demands for healthier products. Similarly, Nintendo products for training the mind and improving mental sharpness were clearly targeted at older buyers, as the company tried to exploit the market opportunity presented by the ageing UK population. Sindy dolls were revamped to give them a new position in the market compared with competitors such as Barbie and Bratz. The strategy was not to face the competitors head on but to redesign Sindy to target younger children.

Some markets, for example computers, require continual updating of their products. One of the first mass-market computers was the IBM 5150, which celebrated its 25th birthday in 2006. So much has changed since the launch of the IBM 5150 in terms of computing power, features and design. Who would have imagined 25 years ago that we would be buying holidays, books, cars and music by computer?

Not all marketing decisions are defensive and the case of Magners cider shows how it is still possible to launch a highly successful brand. The cider market was assumed to be relatively stagnant until Magners' recent promotional success, which led to a doubling of production capacity. This highlights how interrelated the different business functions are: the effectiveness of the product's marketing required a change in the firm's operations.

Of course, generating sales lies at the heart of much of marketing, but this does not necessarily mean that firms always want to sell more. High sales can sometimes devalue a brand, as Ford believed was the case with its Mondeo and, more recently, its Taurus model in the USA. Being too accessible means that the price of a product may have to be reduced to reflect its lower brand status, which could make it less desirable to future buyers. Although Burberry has been hugely successful in broadening its market appeal, continued growth of sales could reduce demand for the brand. The prospect of increased sales did not stop Tyrrells Potato Chips from asking Tesco not to stock its crisps in the supermarket's stores (a result of Tesco's earlier dealings with Tyrrells' owner, William Chase).

Marketing can sometimes be too effective in generating sales. For example, the Carphone Warehouse found that so many customers wanted to take up its TalkTalk promotion for 'free' broadband that it could not easily fulfil the orders. Slow response times threatened the company's hard-earned reputation for good customer service.

The value of a brand was shown in 2006, when Ford paid £6 million for the Rover name.

Some marketing decisions are part of an overall corporate strategy to broaden a company's offerings — for example, Marks and Spencer announced a move into electrical goods in 2006. A company must decide how to expand its range in a way that fits with the overall approach of the business — what level of service to provide, what range and brands to stock, or what price to set.

Organic foods

Sales of organic products in the UK are now worth around £1.6 billion a year and constitute a rapidly growing segment of the food market. All the major supermarkets are expanding their organic range of products. Five years ago, sales were only around £1.2 billion. Originally, demand was particularly high in affluent areas and in stores with higher-income customers (e.g. Waitrose). Asda has been slow to react to this trend, but in 2006 it expanded its range rapidly to around 1,000 organic product lines.

Not all organic farmers are pleased with these developments. The big super-markets insist that products display their own brand labels and they also drive down prices, thus forcing the smaller farmers out of business.

Q4.1 Why do you think that sales of organic products are increasing?

Coke Zero

Reacting to increased consumer interest in healthier drinks, Coca-Cola brought out Coke Zero in the summer of 2006. Supported by a huge marketing campaign and benefiting from hot weather, initial sales were high. The product is aimed at young men, a demographic group that tends to avoid diet drinks. The success of Coke Zero was vitally important to Coca-Cola because of the changing demands of consumers and a move away from high-sugar carbonated drinks. Pepsi had already diversified into healthier soft drinks and water products, and Coca-Cola was criticised for being slow to react. Its previous attempt to enter these markets ended in disaster in 2004 when it had to withdraw its water, Dasani, from the shelves. This was because of a contamination scare and also the reaction of consumers when they discovered that Dasani was processed tap water. Coca-Cola's other brands in the UK include Sprite, Dr Pepper, Powerade and Oasis.

Q4.2 What factors are likely to determine the long-term success of Coke Zero?

Computer games for older buyers

Although usually associated with teenage buyers, computer games are now being targeted at older consumers. Nintendo has sold over 5 million copies of its Dr Kawashima brain-training games since this product range was launched in Japan in 2005. The games, which provide a daily regime of brain-enhancing exercises, were launched in the UK in 2006. Activities include basic maths problems and reading and counting exercises. Your result is given as a brain age. Unlike Donkey Kong or Mario, Dr Kawashima does exist and is a brain researcher based at Tohoku University in Japan. The games will be advertised in *Saga Magazine*, a publication that provides services for older readers.

Q4.3 How might Nintendo alter its marketing in order to target older buyers?

New-look Sindy

In 2006, the Sindy doll was relaunched after a £3 million makeover. The new look was a return to the doll's appearance in the early 1960s — younger and less curvaceous. The new Sindy drives a mini to show her Britishness and is targeted more at younger buyers than Barbie. Sindy is owned by Devon-based firm Pedigree Toys. Originally the company licensed Sindy to Hasbro, but 5 years ago it bought back the rights and decided to relaunch the doll.

Q4.4 How has the marketing of Barbie been changed in order to maintain sales over the years?

Happy Birthday IBM 5150!

The 25th anniversary of the launch of the IBM 5150 computer was celebrated in 2006. The arrival of this product is recognised by many as a turning point in the development of the personal-computer (PC) market, because it started the growth of home computers. At a cost of $1,565, the IBM 5150 had 16 kilobytes of memory and used cassettes to load and save data. The subsequent growth in PC usage has been huge and there are approximately 1 billion PCs worldwide. According to *The Economist*, there are 70 PCs per 100 people in the USA, 35 in France, 7 in Brazil and 3 in China. The impact of computers on our lives and on business activity is extraordinary. They have revolutionised how we store and manipulate data and communicate, helping us to process data more quickly and make better decisions. PCs have also improved productivity significantly.

Although other machines were available when the 5150 was brought out, it achieved great success because of the IBM brand name and its low price. IBM kept the cost down by using off-the-shelf components rather than specially designed parts. The machine contained a microprocessor from Intel and software from Microsoft (which has gone on to dominate the software industry). The 5150 established the PC as a valuable asset for both business and the home.

However, the world continues to change as a result of technological developments. In July 2006, the chief software architect of Microsoft, Ray Ozzie, stated that the dominance of the PC was now over. Ozzie said that in the past Microsoft had had a PC mindset, but now the company was in a new era in which the internet was at the centre of its thinking and planning. Although the PC is far from dead, the future of computing lies in mobile phones, digital media players, games consoles and television set-top boxes. Microsoft has already entered these arenas, selling 30 million Xbox games consoles, 6 million mobile phones based on the Windows operating system and 14 million PCs that act as media centres when linked to televisions. Meanwhile, Apple has sold over 50 million iPods and Sony has sold over 100 million PlayStation 2 consoles.

Q4.5 What are the most significant technological changes in today's computing market?

Magners

C&C is the Irish drinks company that owns the Magners brand. In 2006, it announced an investment of £135 million in its Clonmel cider factory. This increased its capacity for the second time in just over 1 year and was a result of the massive rise in demand for the Magners brand. Production capacity is around 500 million litres a year.

Since its initial launch in Northern Ireland 4 years ago, Magners' sales have increased rapidly. In the first half of 2006, sales increased 250%, in part owing to the warm summer. This success encouraged imitators: brewer Scottish & Newcastle launched a new cider product called Sirrus and also produced a pint-bottle version of Bulmers Original. C&C said that it was not achieving growth through discounts; in fact, profit margins were increasing.

Q4.6 What are the dangers of doubling capacity?

No Tyrrells at Tesco

In 2006, Tesco had to agree to not stock products from crisp manufacturer Tyrrells Potato Chips. Tyrrells is a producer of upmarket crisps and is based

in Herefordshire. Tesco had bought its supplies of the crisps from a wholesaler without Tyrrells knowing. Tyrrells threatened to sue Tesco if it carried on selling the products. The crisps are sold by 6,000 independent retailers and Waitrose. The company said it would rather work with and support its direct customers. (It was prepared to deal with Waitrose because of its good reputation in dealing with suppliers.) The owner of Tyrrells, William Chase, said that he was forced to abandon his potato business 6 years ago because large supermarkets, led by Tesco, began buying potatoes overseas to bring down costs. Therefore, he would not now be willing to sell his crisps to them.

The Competition Commission has stated that the relationship between super-markets and their suppliers is one of the key areas that it wants to investigate in an ongoing inquiry into supermarkets. Friends of the Earth said that the investigation might prevent small farmers from being bullied.

Q4.7   Do you think that Tyrrells is right to stop Tesco distributing its crisps?

Carphone Warehouse

In 2006, Carphone Warehouse offered a 'free' broadband service as part of its TalkTalk promotion (it is not completely free — although there is no charge for the broadband service, there is a monthly line rental). Demand was huge and this created a customer-service 'nightmare' according to the company's chief executive, Charlie Dunstone. More than 400,000 customers signed up for high-speed internet access in the first 4 months — far more than expected. The high demand created delays and meant that the company could not deliver its usual level of service. According to Carphone Warehouse, most people would save £250 a year by switching to the TalkTalk offer, but the company had not appreciated just how attractive the offer would be. Following the surge in demand, the need to improve customer service became the company's priority. Dunstone described the broadband business as 'our own little sister, a little baby who's waking up every 2 hours and is disturbing the family and making our lives a nightmare. We must not lose sight of the fact that quite soon she will grow up into a beautiful young girl and we'll love her dearly'. BSkyB responded to the TalkTalk offer 3 months later by launching its own service.

TalkTalk's biggest problem was low call-centre capacity. On average, callers had to wait 3.5 minutes for an answer. The company had 1,550 people working in its call centre but had to recruit even more to boost capacity.

Q4.8   How could a company forecast demand for a new promotional offer?

Ford buys Rover name

The Rover brand is closely associated with British car production. Although the company failed, the brand name is still felt to be valuable. In 2006, Ford bought the rights to the Rover name from BMW for a reported £6 million. Some observers think that Ford will revive old Rover models such as the Vanden Plas, Triumph or Morris. Others think that Ford has bought Rover simply to prevent its competitors from owning it and damaging Ford's Land Rover and Range Rover brands. When MG Rover collapsed, the Longbridge factory, machinery and the right to produce its other car models (e.g. the Wolseley and the Sprite) went to the Chinese car company Nanjing Automobile.

Q4.9 Why should a company pay to buy a brand name?

New products at M&S

Marks and Spencer announced in 2006 that it was going to open electrical departments in almost 100 stores. This was a real blow to DSG International, the owner of Currys and Currys Digital. One week earlier, Tesco had announced that it was increasing its electrical range with the launch of Tesco Direct, a home-shopping service offering more than 8,000 new products. The move also threatened retailer Argos.

Electrical goods will be sold in separate departments in M&S stores by specially trained staff. Products will include DVD players, televisions, hifi systems, camcorders, microwaves, digital radios and mobile and landline telephones in its bigger stores, with a more limited range in smaller shops. The company has done a deal with manufacturers such as Sony, Samsung and Nokia to sell their products in conjunction with the M&S brand. In some cases, M&S has rewritten instruction booklets to make them more user-friendly.

Q4.10 What factors would Marks and Spencer have taken into account before choosing to enter the electrical goods sector?

CoolBrands

The top ten CoolBrands in 2006 according to the *Sunday Times* were:
1 Aston Martin
2 Alexander McQueen
3 iPod
4 Agent Provocateur
5 Bang and Olufsen
6 Google
7 Green and Black's
8 Tate Modern

9 Jimmy Choo
10 Vivienne Westwood

Source: CoolBrands Survey 2006

The brands were rated by 21 'style leaders' according to the extent to which they were 'desirable among...style leaders and influencers' and have 'a magic about them, signifying users have a sense of taste and style'.

Q4.11 What would be your top ten brands?

Chapter 5

Finance

About this chapter

Finance is important in any organisation. Although accountants are sometimes called 'bean counters', they do much more than simply add up how much profit is made. Management accountants advise managers on what decisions to take, the cost and revenue implications of these decisions and whether they are worth the investment. They also control the cashflow of a business by influencing when bills are paid and how long customers are given to pay. In 2006, the DIY company B&Q decided to increase the time taken to pay its suppliers. This would obviously help B&Q's cashflow but not that of its suppliers — this action raises ethical as well as financial issues.

Working out how well a business is performing does involve measuring its profits, but this is only one indicator of success. The accountants of oil company Shell would probably have been pleased with its declared profits of over £13 billion in 2006. However, some analysts criticised Shell, arguing that it could have made even more money.

We also examine the case of Italian dairy company Parmalat, whose accounts turned out to be inaccurate. Even if accounts are audited, it seems as though they cannot always be trusted.

B&Q

In January 2006, B&Q, the DIY store owned by Kingfisher, announced that it was going to double the period taken to pay its suppliers. The DIY industry has been hit by the downturn in consumer spending, forcing firms such as B&Q to review their operations. In the past, B&Q paid its suppliers within 49 days of receiving goods, but its change in policy meant that this period would increase to around 90 days. (The industry average is 45 days.) The company also insisted that suppliers must ask its permission before securing a loan based on outstanding B&Q payments. A B&Q spokesperson said that the changes were aimed at shifting payment from when goods are delivered to when they are sold. Before this announcement, B&Q's performance had been poor; some analysts said that the business had been distracted by its overseas expansion and had neglected its domestic operations.

In July 2006, Kingfisher announced a £200-million refurbishment of its 110 biggest B&Q warehouse outlets. The chief executive also called a halt to

further overseas expansion. Instead, the company will concentrate on regions in which it already operates (e.g. France, Poland, China and Russia).

Ian Cheshire, who took over as chief executive in 2004, has already cut 400 jobs and plans to close 17 stores as part of a restructuring plan.

Q5.1 What might be the consequences of B&Q's decision to double the number of days taken to pay its suppliers?

Shell's record profits

The increase in world oil prices in 2005 helped Royal Dutch Shell to achieve a record annual profit for a UK public company of $22.94 billion (£13.12 billion) in 2006. However, despite this success, some analysts argue that Shell needs to plan more for the future and invest in research and development. Critics point also to the fact that Shell's reserve/replacement ratio (the capacity to replace pumped oil with new oil) was 70–80%. A rate of more than 100% is usually needed to keep asset bases solid. Shell is drilling for oil in Australia, Brazil, Brunei, Egypt, Germany, Malaysia, the Netherlands, Nigeria, Oman, the UK and the USA.

Q5.2 Do you think that Shell's profits are impressive?

Parmalat

In 2006, one of the world's biggest corporate fraud trials began in Italy. The former boss and founder of Parmalat, a dairy company, and 15 others are accused of fixing the price of milk and providing false accounting information. Thousands of investors lost money when Parmalat was declared bankrupt in 2004. This followed an admission that a company bank account containing nearly €4 billion (held in the Cayman Islands) did not exist. A letter from the Bank of America in the Cayman Islands confirming that the account existed appears to have been forged. This prompted an investigation into the company's finances and it was discovered that Parmalat had a debt of around €14 billion — eight times more than had been reported officially. It is suspected that the company misled investors by making up contracts in order to borrow money to finance expansion. Parmalat is now run by an administrator appointed by the Italian government. As a result of the scandal, shares in the company, which had been worth €1.8 billion, became worthless. Most of the company will be sold off to pay creditors.

Q5.3 Can corporate fraud ever be prevented completely?

Chapter 6

Human resource management

About this chapter

'People are the key to our business' is a claim made by many organisations and in many cases it is true. Employees deal with customers, provide products, solve problems and come up with innovations. Therefore, managing people effectively can increase a firm's competitiveness. The role of employees is particularly important with the rise of the service sector in the UK. Over the last 9 years, the number of people working in the UK service industry has increased by around 20%; the number employed in manufacturing has fallen by 30%. Services rely heavily on the quality of staff.

The need to attract good staff is demonstrated by McDonald's drive to raise the status of jobs in the company. McDonald's emphasised the opportunities for career development and the range of benefits available for what are sometimes perceived as basic jobs. It also introduced a scheme to enable staff to gain qualifications at work — an important step when some skills are in short supply. Enabling employees to become more qualified may also motivate them, which is important because staff satisfaction can make or break a business.

The dangers of having a discontented workforce were highlighted in 2006 when many council employees went on strike. Strikes mean lost output and a poor level of service. The council dispute was over pensions — an increasingly important issue for business. Many firms have committed themselves to pension schemes that are now unaffordable because of increased life expectancies. This is leading to major changes in promises to future staff and, in some cases, to existing staff as well.

Keeping staff motivated is not just about financial rewards. Employees need to feel involved in the business and part of the decision-making process. In a famously blunt e-mail at a division of HSBC, one manager demonstrated how not to keep staff motivated by calling into question the management style in his department. In contrast, if you worked at investment bank Goldman Sachs, the financial rewards would be so high that you might be willing to put up with most behaviour. The gap between such high earners and those on the minimum wage is great, but some people think that the minimum wage is too high and that it causes unemployment.

Working for McDonald's

McDonald's launched a promotional campaign in 2006 to improve its image as an employer. It ran a poster campaign under the slogan 'Not bad for a McJob', with the aim of changing people's perceptions of what it is like to work for the

firm. The company's vice-president in the UK said: 'A huge gap exists between the external perception and the internal reality of working for McDonald's. The simple fact is, our employer reputation is not justified.' The fast-food chain employs 78,000 workers at 1,250 outlets and spends £14 million a year on training. Other key facts about McDonald's include the following:

- More than half of McDonald's senior and middle-ranking executives started work in its restaurants as hourly paid 'crew members' and were promoted internally.
- About 20% of the company's franchisees also started off working there. McDonald's offers various schemes to help staff to raise the £250,000 investment typically needed to become a franchisee of the company.
- Staff can work flexible hours to allow them to care for their children, the sick or elderly. Parents can work school hours and students can work around university and college term times.
- More than 80% of McDonald's UK staff earn more than the minimum wage; half of the company's managers earn £40,000 a year or more.
- After 3 years of service, employees are offered free private health care for themselves, their spouses and dependent children. For every 10 years of service, staff members are entitled to an 8-week paid sabbatical. This is in addition to 4 weeks' annual paid holiday, which increases to 5 weeks after 3 years.

Last year, McDonald's became an Investor in People. This is an award given by an independent body that sets and measures employment standards. The company is also keen to help employees develop their basic skills and now offers them the chance to gain GCSE-equivalent qualifications at work. The company website will feature information on topics such as becoming a parent or buying a house. All 78,000 staff members will have access to website materials and the support of an online tutor. The exams have been developed by the OCR examination board and can be taken in a training area or staff room.

Q6.1   What are the benefits to McDonald's of improving its image as an employer?

The UK skills shortage

According to the Trade Union Congress (TUC), which represents many unions in the UK, more than one-third of employers offer their workers no training. Nearly 11.5% of those who do get training receive a nationally recognised qualification. The TUC's view is that employers should waste less time complaining about the lack of skills among their staff members and spend more time training them. In the current UK workforce of around 30 million, 6 million people have literacy problems.

Council strike

On 27 March 2006, the retailer John Lewis raised the normal retirement age for its staff from 60 to 65. This change will be phased in for employees in their 40s. This decision was agreed by staff and will allow the firm to keep its retirement scheme in which pensions are based on years of service and final salary. The following day, hundreds of thousands of council workers went on strike to oppose a similar change to the local government scheme. Public transport was disrupted and schools, libraries and sports centres were also affected.

The strike was organised by 11 unions to oppose the abolition of the '85 rule'. This rule means that although 65 is the normal retirement age, employees can stop work at 60 on favourable terms if their age and years of service add up to 85 or more. A worker with 25 years' service could therefore retire at the age of 60. The government argued that the scheme was no longer affordable, as people are living longer.

Q6.3   What determines the power of a trade union in an industrial dispute?

Communication

Below is the text of an e-mail that was sent by the head of global equity research at HSBC to the bank's London analysts.

Gentlemen

I am receiving calls of complaint from the sales and trading desks in London on a daily basis about the lack of product in London. We have dropped from what was an unacceptably low average of 30 pieces of research a week across Europe to a number that is less than half this average...

THIS IS COMPLETELY UNACCEPTABLE.

No good analyst needs to be pushed like this — most are self-motivated and interested in driving their external values...As team leaders and managers you have to take responsibility for your teams and for their motivation and production levels — this is what we pay you for...team leaders do not deserve to be paid this year...take some responsibility and push your teams.

Q6.4   How do think that this e-mail would affect the employees who received it?

Goldman Sachs

The investment bank Goldman Sachs declared record profits of over $4.7 billion for the first half of 2006. The company, which employs around 24,000 staff, is known for the high rewards that if offers in salaries and bonuses. In 2006, its employees were paid, on average, over $500,000 each! Not surprisingly, demand for jobs there is fiercely competitive.

Q6.5 Can such high levels of pay be justified?

Minimum wages may cause job losses

According to the British Retail Consortium (September 2006), the national minimum wage had led to a loss of 78,000 jobs. It also claimed that more jobs were likely to be lost when the minimum wage increased from £5.05 to £5.35 an hour later in the year. However, some unions claimed that employers were simply looking for ways of holding back pay increases. Moreover, the Transport and General Workers' Union (TGWU) argued that the minimum wage should be increased to £6 an hour.

Q6.6 Is there a need for the minimum wage?

Chapter 7

Operations

About this chapter

Some people believe that marketing is all-important — without customers there is no business. However, operations may claim to be the most important part of a business (if any one function can be more significant than another).

Operations is the function that provides the products — without products, there is nothing to sell to customers. Operations management affects costs, quality, level of service and flexibility, so it can be an important source of competitive advantage. Where you are based, what you offer, how you produce it and what you use are all significant contributors to a firm's success.

Problems with a product (e.g. delays in the development of the Airbus or PlayStation 3) can lead to dissatisfied customers, cancelled orders and loss of future business. In the case of Cadbury in 2006, some of its chocolate products became contaminated and had to be recalled. Managing such a crisis does not involve just short-term issues. The products have to be withdrawn quickly (imagine having to manage the recall of over 1 million chocolate bars), but the brand has to be protected for the long term. Cadbury has pursued a policy of master branding, which means that all its products carry the Cadbury name and logo (unlike Mars, for example). The company could be badly affected if customers lose faith in the quality of its products.

The Dell announcement in 2006 that it is to open factories in India is a strategic operational decision that will affect its costs and ability to deliver quickly to local markets.

Waiting for an Airbus

In June 2006, Airbus reported long delays for deliveries of its A380 airliner, an aircraft that can seat 555 people. Following the announcement, the value of shares in Airbus's parent company, EADS, fell 26% in 1 day, wiping almost $7 billion (€5.5 billion) off the value of the business. The statement about the delays came after Airbus had already extended its delivery deadline by 6 months earlier in the year. Even before these announcements, orders were slowing up — a worry when the company needs to recover €12 billion of research and development costs. One major problem is that the waiting time for an A380 is 6 years.

Airbus has sold 159 of the $250 million jets to 16 airlines, including Emirates, Virgin, Air France and Qantas, many of which are likely to demand penalties for late delivery of the aircraft. This is a significant reversal of fortune for the

company. For much of the decade up to 2004/05, Airbus performed better than its main rival Boeing and outsold it in 6 of the last 7 years.

| Q7.1 | How might Airbus be affected by the delays in supplying its A380 aircraft? |

Sony launch delayed

In late 2006, Sony announced delays to the launch of its next generation PlayStation 3 (PS3) video games console in Europe, Asia and Australia until March 2007. This postponement led gamers to switch to other products, such as Microsoft's Xbox 360. The delay affected games companies that had released PS3 games ready for Christmas and also impacted on sales of Sony's new high-definition DVD format called Blu-ray. The PS3 incorporates a built-in Blu-ray disc player and it was expected to give a major boost to Christmas sales of this new format. Instead, sales were lost to Toshiba and Microsoft, which launched an add-on high-definition DVD player for the Xbox 360 before Sony. The Blu-ray technology is said to be superior to the Toshiba version but it is more difficult to manufacture, which might have caused the PS3 delay.

PlayStation 3 was finally launched in Japan in November 2006, but supplies were limited to less than 100,000 units. The US launch followed soon after, but less than 175,000 units were available there. Not surprisingly, long queues formed outside the shops on the day PS3 was released. Thousands of people had camped outside some stores in the USA.

| Q7.2 | If possible, should Sony have launched its product, even if it had faults? |

Cadbury recall

Following fears over salmonella contamination of its chocolate, Cadbury had to recall more than 1 million bars. The contamination was thought to be due to a leaking pipe at Cadbury's Marlbrook plant, near Leominster in Herefordshire. The problem was first discovered in January 2006 and samples were sent to an independent laboratory for testing. The government's Health Protection Agency (HPA) confirmed that the samples contained a form of salmonella, and the Food Standards Agency (FSA) was alerted. Although the levels of contamination were significantly below the amount needed to cause any health problems, the products were recalled as a precaution.

The factory at Marlbrook processes 180 million litres of fresh milk, 56,000 tonnes of sugar and 13,000 tonnes of cocoa to produce 97,000 tonnes of milk chocolate crumb every year. This product is transported to other sites at Bournville (near Birmingham) and Somerdale (near Bristol) and is mixed with cocoa butter and turned into milk chocolate.

Other famous recalls include:

- Premier Foods' withdrawal of Worcester sauce and Branston pickle products that were contaminated with a dye called Sudan 1 (2005)
- Nestlé's recall of baby milk in continental Europe because the products were contaminated by chemicals used in the packaging (late 2005)
- Heinz's withdrawal of eight varieties of baby food that were wrongly labelled (2003)
- Coca-Cola's recall of millions of cans of its drinks in France, Belgium, the Netherlands and Luxembourg after people complained of stomach pains (1999)
- Perrier's recall of bottles of mineral water after traces of benzene were found in them (1990)

Cadbury identified salmonella in its products in January but did not tell the government until June. The company had used its own criteria and decided that the threat to the public was non-existent. Following the salmonella scare, Cadbury's market share fell 1.1% to 31.3%. It intends to spend £5 million on rebuilding the brand. The UK confectionery business accounts for about 13% of the Cadbury group's sales.

Q7.3 What are the possible consequences of this recall for Cadbury?

New location for Dell

In 2006, Dell announced that it will open its first manufacturing plant in India, which will focus on making desktop computers. The company said that India offers an exceptional workforce and a good strategic investment zone. Locating in India would avoid taxes that have to be paid when exporting into the country. It would also reduce delivery time and costs.

Q7.4 What other factors might influence a company's decision about where to locate?

Chapter 8

Competition

About this chapter

The degree of competition in a market can have a significant effect on the success and likely rewards of a business. Apple's spectacular success with the iPod attracted many imitators into the market in 2006.

Although greater competition will threaten sales, how firms compete with each other is also important. In some cases, competition can be ferocious, leading to anticompetitive behaviour by some companies. This occurs when businesses act against the public interest — for example, organisations may work together to raise prices or a company could deliberately sell products at a loss in order to force a rival out of business. If anticompetitive behaviour is suspected, a government agency called the Office of Fair Trading can investigate and it has the power to fine guilty companies.

In 2006, a high-profile investigation began when the head offices of British Airways (BA) were raided. BA was alleged to have colluded with other airlines to increase prices. In a separate investigation, several firms involved in supplying copper fittings were found guilty of colluding and abusing monopoly power.

Apple's iPod

Apple's sales of iPods (personal music players) have been exceptional since the product was launched. In the last 3 months of 2005, Apple sold more than 14 million iPods. However, sales of its computers were unexpectedly low, at just 1.25 million during the same period. The Apple Mac computer has historically been the main earner for the business. This may not continue and some analysts are concerned that Apple is becoming too dependent on the iPod. In total, approximately 42 million iPods were sold between 2001 and the start of 2006. Apple is facing increased competition from imitators such as Samsung's YM-P1 player and Creative Labs' Zen Vision.

Q8.1 Do you think that Apple can protect itself from its competitors?

Allegations of price-fixing at BA

In June 2006, the Office of Fair Trading (OFT) began an investigation into claims of price-fixing at the head offices of British Airways (BA) in an attempt to find out whether BA had colluded with other airlines in setting its fuel surcharges. Over the last few years, airlines have added surcharges to ticket prices to compensate for the increasing cost of aviation fuel. If BA is found guilty, the OFT could fine it up to 10% of its £850-million turnover.

The OFT is also carrying out a criminal investigation, which means that any individual found guilty could be imprisoned for up to 5 years. The airline suspended two senior executives after the investigation began in June. Virgin Atlantic, American Airlines and United Airlines assisted in the inquiry into the existence of a cartel.

The head of campaigns at the Consumer Association welcomed the investigation and hoped that if evidence of collusion was found, 'tough sanctions are made in order to send a clear signal to business that price-fixing will not be tolerated'. News of the alleged collusion sent BA shares, which had been trading at a 5-year high, down 6% to 346p.

Q8.2   Why might the airlines have colluded? Why should the Office of Fair Trading investigate such allegations?

UK cartel firms fined

In 2006, five UK firms were among 30 companies that were fined a total of over £211 million by the European Commission for their part in a copper-fittings cartel. The UK companies involved were Tomkins, Delta, IMI, Advanced Fluid Connections (AFC) and Flowflex. These firms colluded to increase the price of copper fittings used in plumbing and heating jobs. Tomkins was fined £3.6 million, Delta £19 million, IMI £32.5 million, AFC £12.16 million and Flowflex £907,736. Another member of the cartel, Mueller, was initially fined £6.9 million, but the company eventually received immunity because it provided information about the collusion.

Q8.3   Should cartel members receive immunity if they provide information about collusions?

Chapter 9

International business

About this chapter

Few firms operate solely in the UK or buy all their supplies within the country. We live in a global economy, buying in supplies and products from all over the world and often selling them abroad as well. This means that the success of most UK firms is dependent on economies worldwide. For example, a boom in the USA can boost UK exports to the USA, whereas an increase in wages in China can raise the costs of imports into the UK. The success of a business abroad will also depend on the effectiveness of its international marketing strategy.

In 2006, Aga, the company that makes premium cookers, announced excellent results, reflecting a well-organised and focused international marketing campaign; further expansion is likely. Tesco is also eager to exploit overseas markets and entered the US market in 2006 by planning to open convenience stores in California. Other companies struggled in overseas markets. Despite its huge economic power, Wal-Mart found that it could not gain sufficient rewards in Germany and decided to pull out.

Aga

One company that did particularly well in 2006 was Aga Foodservice. Best known for its upmarket cookers, Aga experienced rapid overseas demand that increased its half-year profits to record levels. Over 30% of its sales now come from abroad. Aga has stores across Europe and is now breaking into the Australian and Chinese markets. It is also looking to develop its key overseas markets further in France and the USA.

Q9.1 What factors might influence overseas demand for Aga cookers?

Tesco enters the US market

In 2006, Tesco announced that it was going to enter the US food market. In 2005 it had sent a group of directors to the USA to find out how consumers there liked to shop. Their aim was to understand how Americans lived and what market opportunities this created. During their stay, they lived with Californian families and kept diaries of their hosts' eating habits, shopping routines, and entertainment and recreation interests. Tesco also built a dummy store in a warehouse and invited over 200 focus groups to tour it and provide feedback.

On the basis of this research, Tesco decided to open a chain of convenience stores in the Express format. This puts Tesco head to head with niche retailers such as Trader Joe's, rather than with the bigger stores of Wal-Mart.

Tesco Express has proved to be a huge success not just in the UK but around the world. The first Express store was opened in the UK in 1994; 2 years later there were only three, but now there are over 800 worldwide. While the underlying approach remains the same, there are significant differences between the stores. In Thailand, the bestselling products include chicken livers and feet and a 200-baht (£3) bucket of food and toiletries for customers who want to give gifts to Buddhist monks. In the UK, a typical Tesco Express is 3,000 sq ft, but in Korea and Malaysia there are stores of up to 10,000 sq ft.

According to commercial estate agents in California, Tesco is looking for stores in Los Angeles between 10,000 sq ft and 12,000 sq ft, with parking for 70 cars and a population of 15,000 in the immediate area. The company is also building a 1.4 million sq ft distribution centre that could service up to 350 stores.

The US launch is expected to cost £250 million but it is not guaranteed to succeed. Many other UK retailers (e.g. Dixons, Marks and Spencer and Sainsbury) have entered this market and failed. The fact that the share price fell when the strategy was first announced shows that some Tesco investors have yet to be convinced.

Q9.2 Why do you think that Tesco wants to expand overseas? Why has it chosen the USA?

Wal-Mart withdrawal

In July 2006, Wal-Mart, the world's biggest retailer, sold its 85 German stores to the German retailer Metro. This brought to an end 8 years of losses incurred as Wal-Mart tried to break into the German market. Earlier in the year, Wal-Mart had already announced that it was pulling out of South Korea.

Wal-Mart entered the German market in 1997, when it bought two existing hypermarket chains. However, it struggled against local competitors such as Aldi and Lidl. In 2005, its sales in Germany were about $2.5 billion compared with global sales of $312 billion. Wal-Mart had difficulties in dealing with the unions in Germany, and local employment laws made it hard to keep costs low. It also struggled to adapt to the German market's needs. In Germany, where domestic 'value retailers' already dominate the grocery market, Wal-Mart found that customers were turned off by its store designs and layouts; German consumers also felt that its product range was too narrow.

According to Wal-Mart's vice-chairman, Michael Duke, the German market was already highly competitive and Wal-Mart was unable to generate the

economies of scale that it needed in order to drive prices below those of its competitors.

Wal-Mart has 2,700 stores in 14 countries outside the USA, representing 40% of the group's total stores, but only 20% of revenue. Further expansion overseas is likely, but not in Germany.

Q9.3   Do you think that Wal-Mart should stop its overseas expansion?

Chapter 10

Legislation

About this chapter

The legal environment can have a significant effect on a firm's performance. Laws can limit what a business can do and what it can sell. They can also affect a firm's costs. Laws can protect firms and individuals from the actions of others.

Gambling is illegal in many US states, so allowing Americans access to online casinos and poker websites could have legal implications. In fact, in 2006, the online gambling industry came under threat from this legislation and two company directors were arrested. If they are found guilty, other firms will be deterred from entering the market, despite the huge profits available.

Legislative action is also affecting car producers in the USA, which have been accused of harming the environment by the state of California. The state is seeking damages from the automotive companies.

Pepsi and Coca-Cola were also involved in legal action in 2006 — their products were banned in the Indian state of Kerala because of alleged safety problems.

Online gambling

In recent years there has been a marked increase in online gambling. Companies operating in this area have benefited from the boom and some have taken the opportunity to float and become public companies. However, the legal status of these businesses has been called into question under US law. In the USA, gambling is strictly controlled and is illegal in many states. Although there was a danger that the US government could take action, most investors felt this not to be a major threat. However, in July 2006, the online gambling industry was shocked when the chief executive of BetonSport was arrested en route to Costa Rica. His plane stopped to refuel in Dallas, where he was arrested by the FBI. The market value of the company fell quickly by 20% and trading in the firm's shares was soon suspended. The company then announced that it was complying with US regulators and stopped 85% of its business, leaving only its Asian websites operational. In September 2006, the chairman of UK-based online gaming firm Sportingbet was also arrested in New York, accused of 'gambling by computer'. In a statement to the London Stock Exchange, Sportingbet stated that it was continuing to operate as normal, including accepting bets from the USA. Sportingbet also owns the Paradise Poker brand and has over 2.5 million registered customers and an annual turnover greater than $1.2 billion (£630 million) — about 70% of its profits are generated in the USA.

Under the Wire Act in the USA, it is illegal for a business to take bets on a sporting contest over any form of wire communication. The relevance of the Act to non-sports gambling such as poker is unclear, but this uncertainty is unsettling for the whole online industry. The US government has also proposed a law banning banks and credit-card companies from processing internet gambling payments. Most operators are based outside the USA, which should mean that they can continue operating as long as their managers do not enter the USA.

The main online betting companies are:
- PartyGaming — this company floated in 2006. It is based in Gibraltar and runs casino sites such as PartyPoker.com. It reported pre-tax profits of $558 million (£300 million) in 2006.
- 888 Holdings — this company runs 888.com, which is based in Gibraltar.
- BetonSport — this group operates from Costa Rica.
- Sportingbet
- Ladbrokes
- William Hill
- Betfair
- Sporting Index

Q10.1 Would you take the risk of investing in an online gambling company given the current legal uncertainty?

Legal action against car companies

In late 2006, the US state of California initiated proceedings to sue the six largest carmakers for their contributions to global warming. Ford, General Motors, Toyota, Honda, Chrysler and Nissan were accused of creating a 'public nuisance' costing millions of dollars. The state claims that these companies have made a major contribution to global warming and should be held responsible for the cost of dealing with the effects. California is the largest car market in the USA, with over 2 million new vehicles registered each year (in the UK, the number is about 2.5 million). Led by Governor Arnold Schwarzenegger, California is trying to reduce the environmental impact of cars. In 2004, the state passed a law to reduce carbon dioxide emissions by 30%. There have already been similar cases in which US states have taken legal action against businesses:
- In 1998, New Orleans sued gunmakers in order to make them pay for the police and hospital costs that arose from use of their weapons. Chicago sued 22 firearms manufacturers for selling guns that they knew were likely to end up in criminal hands.
- In the late 1990s, large numbers of smokers in Florida sued the five biggest cigarette manufacturers for the damage caused by smoking; they won £76 billion, although this decision was later revoked.

- In 2002, a man from New York sued McDonald's, Wendy's, KFC and Burger King for damages on the grounds that their products had made him obese.

Q10.2 What are the likely effects of the legal action by the state of California against major car companies?

Pepsi and Coca-Cola

In 2006, Pepsi and Coca-Cola won a legal battle to overturn a ban on their products in the southern Indian state of Kerala. A court ruled that the ban imposed in August was 'harsh, unjust and arbitrary'. (It was based on a report that suggested that the drinks contained harmful pesticides.) The ban meant that a market of up to 30 million potential customers was closed, but it had been introduced without any independent verification of the products' quality. The companies said that the ingredients used to make their fizzy drinks conformed to the highest purity standards.

Q10.3 What other external factors, apart from the law, might affect the success of Pepsi or Coca-Cola?

Chapter 11

Technology

About this chapter

Technological developments drive change: new products, new markets, different ways of doing business, new methods of producing and delivering products, different ways of communicating, marketing and even measuring performance. In 2006, the opportunities created by the internet continued to become apparent. Rupert Murdoch's News Corporation, which owns numerous magazines, newspapers and television stations worldwide (e.g. the *Sun*, *The Times* and Sky in the UK) became more involved in new media. Recently it bought MySpace and in 2006 moved into the mobile-phone download business, opening up many new opportunities.

The sale of YouTube to Google for £1.65 billion demonstrates the value of online business.

Another interesting technological development is the introduction of online stamps, which removes the need to buy books of stamps from post offices and shops.

Rupert Murdoch and the Crazy Frog

Rupert Murdoch's News Corporation spent over $187 million (£100 million) in 2006 in buying a 51% share of the company that developed the highly successful Crazy Frog ringtone. The company is called Jamba, but it trades in the UK and the USA as Jamster. Last year, News Corporation also bought the social networking site MySpace. It plans to integrate Jamba with its Mobizzo mobile content business, which is creating shows designed specifically for mobile phones. News Corporation's president said, 'This is an important step in News Corp's strategy of becoming the world's leading digital media company.' The new business will also be used to launch a MySpace mobile store selling ringtones and wallpapers to MySpace users. Companies that make shows are increasingly excited by the idea of selling to mobile-phone users. There are more mobile-phone owners than computer owners. Although ringtones are likely to remain the main product in the short term, video is expected to grow rapidly as technology continues to improve.

Q11.1   Do you think that selling video and film to play on mobile phones is likely to be a big market?

Google and YouTube

In October 2006, Google announced it was buying the video sharing website YouTube for $1.65 billion in shares. It said the two companies would continue to operate independently. YouTube was launched in February 2005 and has grown quickly into one of the most popular websites on the internet. It has around 100 million videos and over 10 million visitors each month. YouTube will keep its brand and its staff, including founders Chad Hurley and Steve Chen. Both companies have recently signed distribution deals to increase the content of the site. YouTube has signed a distribution deal with Universal Music Group and CBS; Google has signed deals with Sony BMG and Warner Music to offer music videos. Google will generate revenue through advertising and selling downloads.

Q11.2   Google has its own video sharing site. Why should it buy YouTube?

Stamps online

Since September 2006, customers have been able to buy stamps online. Postage costs are paid by credit card and customers are given a barcode that can be printed off at home and stuck onto letters, which are then posted in the usual way. The service is available 24 hours a day and is more convenient than queuing for books of stamps. The barcodes can also be printed direct onto envelopes. However, local post offices are already struggling to stay in business and they may find that this new development makes their situation worse.

Q11.3   Do you think that this technology will succeed? Why was it not launched sooner?

Chapter 12

External factors

About this chapter

The performance of a business depends heavily on the external environment. Changes in this environment can affect demand, costs and the degree of competition in a market. In turn, these factors influence a firm's profits and survival. This chapter looks first at the impact of the football World Cup on different organisations. The 2006 World Cup caused major changes in consumer habits — such as what people bought, how much television they watched and how often they went out during that period. Some firms benefited from this (e.g. football-kit manufacturers), but other companies found it harder to attract customers during the big matches. The hot summer of 2006 also affected many businesses. For example, in warmer weather, we may drink more and swim more, but we shop less.

The economy is an important external factor. Businesses need to anticipate future changes in economic factors such as interest rates, inflation and exchange rates. In this chapter, we consider several interesting economic issues. For example, the economy in Zimbabwe performed badly in 2006 and experienced inflation of over 1,000%. Meanwhile, in the UK, the Monetary Policy Committee increased interest rates, which affect a firm's costs and demand. This measure was taken partly to decrease demand — high levels of demand had led to continued increases in house prices. In 2006, the average house price in the UK was nearly £200,000.

One of the most significant global economic changes in 2006 was the increase in oil prices. The substantial rise in the price of oil raised costs and made several investment projects unviable. Other economic changes around the world included the introduction of a tax on wooden chopsticks in China to reduce the number of trees being cut down.

The World Cup effect

The 2006 World Cup had a great impact on business in the UK. In the 3 months before the World Cup began in June, retail sales grew 2.1% compared with the same period in 2005. Consumers brought forward their spending to the period just before the World Cup, so that they would not miss any matches. Other winners and losers during the World Cup included the following businesses:

- Scottish & Newcastle (the brewery company) benefited from the publicity it received during the competition. The company sponsored France, one of the finalists, through its brand Kronenbourg. It also sponsored Portugal (which reached the semifinals) with its brand Sagres. Sales of Scottish & Newcastle's main brands in Britain (Foster's, John Smith's and Strongbow) were also high as England reached the quarterfinals.

- JD Wetherspoon is a chain that does not allow television in its pubs, but it decided to let landlords show matches and even turn up the sound during important games. Sales increased by 5.1% compared with 2005.
- Although pubs reported good sales in June, so did the take-home trade as many Britons chose to watch the games at home. England games often took nearly 80% of the available television audience.
- Sales of retailer Kesa Electricals were boosted by the demand for new televisions, especially flat-screen models, in the run-up to the World Cup. Kesa's businesses include Comet in the UK and Darty and BUT in France.
- Umbro is the official supplier of football kit to the England team. The 2006 top for the tournament in Germany was its best-selling shirt ever. Sales for the first half of the year were £247 million — 41% higher than the same period in 2005. Umbro makes kits for 150 football teams worldwide and has the contract for the England squad until 2014.
- Domino's Pizza benefited from a 25% rise in profits during the World Cup, partly because of advertising campaigns such as Michael Owen's promotion of the Football Fanatic Pizza. Despite such an increase in profits, the company had hoped for more, and attributed the lower figures to the hot weather and England's failure to make the semifinals.

Q12.1 Which other firms would win or lose during a major sporting event?

UK weather

The summer of 2006 was hot — July 2006 was the warmest July on record. The high temperatures drove consumers away from the high street, thus affecting retailers' sales. People preferred leisure activities to going shopping. However, shops with air conditioning performed better than those without. Internet sales also increased during this period.

The heatwave pushed up demand for electricity to power air conditioning units, fans and refrigeration units, resulting in power shortages in some areas.

Q12.2 Which firms might benefit during bad weather?

Economic growth

Table 12.1 lists the predicted GDP growth and inflation rates for some major economies.

	GDP growth (%)	Inflation (%)
USA	3.1	2.4
Eurozone	2.1	2.0
Japan	2.2	0.8
UK	2.9	1.7
China	9.5	3.5
India	7.1	4.3
Russia	5.7	10.0

Source: Organisation for Economic Cooperation and Development

Table 12.1 Predictions for GDP growth and inflation in 2007

Q12.3 How might these predictions help UK firms?

The Big Mac index

The Economist invented the Big Mac index in 1986 as a way of analysing what the values of different currencies should be. The results are compared with actual values to assess whether a currency is over- or undervalued. The idea is simple: a McDonald's Big Mac is a standard product, so the price should be approximately the same around the world. If a Big Mac costs £2.00 in the UK and $3 in the USA, the 'right' exchange rate should be $1.50:£1. This exchange rate would make the burger the same price in both currencies. If the actual exchange rate is $1.88:£1, it would mean that the pound was overvalued. A 'strong' pound means that the pound is relatively expensive, which makes UK exports more expensive in foreign currencies.

On the basis of the Big Mac index in May 2006, *The Economist* came to the following conclusions:
- The Chinese yuan was undervalued by nearly 60% against the dollar. This means that Chinese goods and services seem cheap to Americans, but US goods appear expensive to the Chinese. This may explain why the USA has a massive trade deficit and China has a large trade surplus.
- The pound was overvalued by nearly 20% against the dollar, which would make exporting to the USA more difficult.

Q12.4 What other products could be used to compare prices across countries?

Inflation over 1,000%

In 2006, Zimbabwe's inflation rate increased to over 1,000%, reaching 1,042.9% in April — the highest rate in the world. This meant that everyday goods were about 11 times more expensive in April 2006 than they were 1 year earlier. The country's economy is in a poor state and experiences shortages of most products. With prices rising so fast, business quotations are often valid only for 24 hours.

In January 2006, the Zimbabwean government introduced a Z$50,000 'bearer cheque' as the highest-value currency note. By August this was not enough to buy a copy of a daily newspaper. In an attempt to tackle inflation, the government revalued the currency by taking three zeros off all prices.

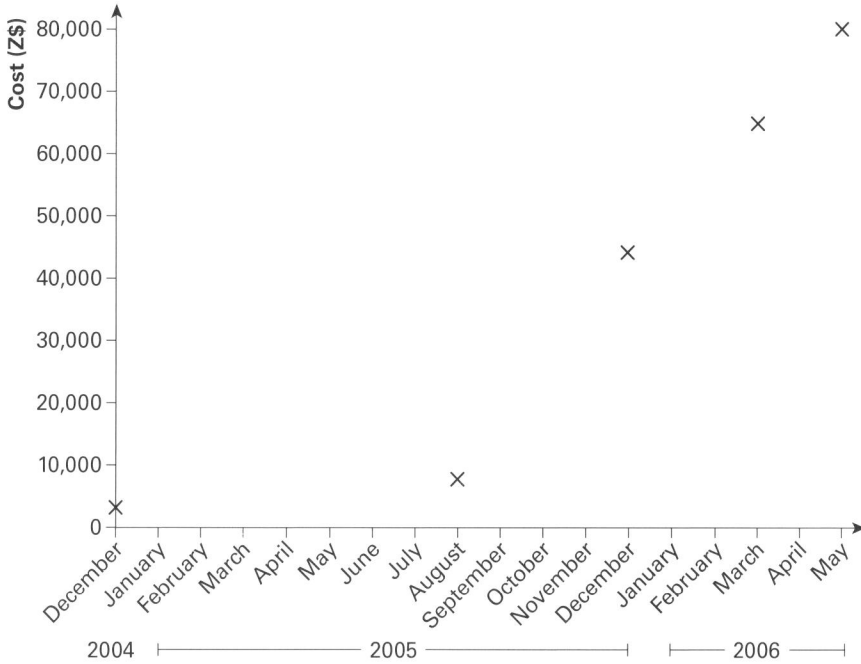

Figure 12.1 The changing price of a loaf of bread in Zimbabwe

---

Q12.5 What might be the consequences of such high inflation for firms trading in, or with, Zimbabwe?

Interest rates

In 2006, the Bank of England increased the interest rate in the UK by 0.25% to 4.75%. All over the world, other central banks raised their interest rates: the European Central bank increased its rate to 3%; in Australia it rose to 6%, while in the USA it was increased 17 times to reach 5.25%. Even Japan, where rates have been close to 0%, experienced an increase in 2006. The logic behind the increases was the fear of inflation. With moderately fast growth in these economies, there were concerns that demand would outstrip supply. Fears over inflation were worsened by oil-price increases, which drove up energy costs. Inflation in the UK rose to 2.5% in 2006, 0.5% higher than the economic target set by the Treasury.

Q12.6 How can an increase in interest rate reduce the rate of inflation?

Budget 2006

Each year, the government presents a budget, setting out its spending plans and how it intends to raise the necessary revenue to finance them. Key points in the 2006 budget included the following:
- Over 5 years, investment in schools will rise from £5.6 billion to £8 billion a year.
- £30 billion of government assets will be sold to finance priorities such as education.
- Tax on cigarettes, wine and beer was increased by 9p, 4p and 1p respectively.
- The personal tax allowance (the level of income that must be reached before tax has to be paid) was raised from £4,895 to £5,035.
- Public pay will rise by 2.25%, on average, in 2007.
- Economic growth is expected to be 2.75–3.25% for 2007/08.

Q12.7 How might businesses benefit from the changes presented in the 2006 budget?

House prices approach £200,000

By June 2006, the average price of a house in England and Wales was around £199,184, nearly 8% higher than in 2005 (see Table 12.2). At the same time, the number of home sales increased by 24% compared with 2005. House price inflation was strongest in the north and northwest, where prices rose by over 11%.

Region	April–June 2005	April–June 2006	Increase (%)
North	124,055	137,861	11.13
Northwest	132,015	146,601	11.05
Yorkshire	133,692	147,230	10.13
Greater London	293,349	317,679	8.29
Wales	138,329	149,063	7.76
West Midlands	155,115	164,576	6.10
Southeast	223,373	236,915	6.06
Southwest	195,496	205,768	5.25
East Midlands	149,683	156,243	4.38
East Anglia	174,929	181,925	4.00

Source: Land Registry

Table 12.2 Average house prices (£) in England and Wales by region

Q12.8 Why do house prices increase? Does it matter if they do?

Oil prices go up

The world price of crude oil went up to over $72 a barrel in 2006 — an increase of more than 18% during the year and a threefold rise over 3 years. This increased costs for firms and created inflationary pressures. The rise in oil prices was due to a number of factors, including:

- the continued rapid growth of the world's biggest economies — China and India — driving up demand for energy
- increased demand for oil in more mature economies (e.g. the USA) to fuel bigger cars and sports utility vehicles.

Overall demand for oil was up by about 1 million barrels a day during 2006. In the next 25 years, it is expected to increase by another 50 million barrels a day to 140 million.

Supply has also been affected — continued attacks in Iraq and security problems in Nigeria have affected the output of these oil-producing countries.

Q12.9 Why does it matter that the price of oil has increased so much?

Poor UK performance

According to the Organisation for Economic Cooperation and Development, the UK needs to make major changes to improve its performance in terms of innovation and productivity. In particular, the UK should focus on:

- the benefits system — to provide a greater incentive to work
- the education system — to provide a better-educated and more skilled workforce
- better transport — to help improve distribution
- health — to provide a fitter workforce
- planning regulations — to enable more firms to compete with existing organisations

The UK's performance in research and development was particularly poor, owing to a lack of funds and too much bureaucracy.

Q12.10 Why is it important for the UK to invest in research and development?

Tax on chopsticks

In an effort to save its forests, the Chinese government introduced a 5% tax on disposable wooden chopsticks. China uses about 45 billion chopsticks a year,

which consume millions of trees and bamboo plants. The government also increased specific taxes to decrease consumption of luxury goods such as yachts, golf clubs and large cars and to reduce differences in income levels. Although the Chinese economy has been growing fast, an estimated 200 million Chinese still live on less than $1 a day.

Q12.11 What taxes would you impose to help protect the environment?

Chapter 13

Strategy

About this chapter

Corporate objectives set out what an organisation wants to achieve. A strategy details how an objective might be met. Adopting the right strategy is fundamental to the success of a business. Strategic decisions determine what products a firm will offer, which markets it will compete in and how it will compete. These decisions usually involve heavy investment and high levels of risk, so they can be difficult to reverse if they go wrong. Launching products in new markets, taking over competitors or redefining the business purpose are all strategic decisions. Companies have to modify their strategies in response to changes in the market or competitors' actions.

In 2006, several companies, including Dell, Vodafone and Ford, rethought their strategies. These companies were struggling despite past successes and took steps to improve performance. Turnaround is certainly possible, as shown by the case of the Piaggio scooter company. Meanwhile, some rival firms joined together to gain strength (Portman and Nationwide announced their proposed merger) and the road haulage company Eddie Stobart moved into new business areas.

Of course, there are many different ways of achieving the same objective. In this chapter, we look at the strategies of Marks and Spencer and Debenhams — both are successful, but they operate differently.

The decline of Dell

Dell was set up in 1984 by Michael Dell in his dormitory room at the University of Texas. The company focused on online selling rather than using retailers and developed a flexible approach to production that aimed to reduce the need for human intervention. For many years, this business approach brought Dell great success and other firms have tried to imitate it. However, in 2006, Dell's share price was in decline and investors became unsure of its future success. Although Dell remains the largest seller of PCs in the world, producing 37 million machines a year and having a market share of over 20%, it is now under threat.

One of the company's main problems lies in what was once its strength: the lack of a retail distribution network. In the past, Dell's lean approach to production, its lack of sales staff and the absence of a direct link to customers enabled it to keep prices lower than those of its rivals. But over the last year,

despite continued price cuts, it failed to gain market share. Other companies have also managed to cut their component costs and have caught up with Dell. Moreover, the main market growth is in the consumer segment rather than the business market (in which Dell sells around 85% of its machines).

Increasing direct sales to customers is difficult for Dell precisely because it does not sell through retail outlets. Customers often want to buy from a shop where they can see the product, talk to sales staff and ask for their advice. Dell cannot offer these services because of its direct-sales model.

Dell may also be suffering because of its insistence on using only Intel chips, rather than rival products from AMD. AMD products are often cheaper and in some cases perform better.

Q13.1 Do you think that it would be wise for Dell to start selling its computers through retail outlets?

M&S and Debenhams

In 2003, the shareholders of Debenhams (Britain's second largest department store) sold the business to private investors — Texas Capital, CVC Capital and Merrill Lynch Global Private Equity — for £600 million (38% more than the shares were worth before the bid). This purchase was worth about four times more by 2006.

Meanwhile, the shareholders of Marks and Spencer held on to their shares when Philip Green made a bid for the company in 2003. Its share price has risen by almost two-thirds since Stuart Rose was hired as the new chief executive 2 years ago. The market value of the company has increased by around £2 billion.

Although both companies have done well, their success has been achieved in different ways. At Debenhams over the last 3 years, managers have increased sales by 15% and increased its share of the department-store market from 15% to 19% (according to Verdict market research). Its operating profit margins have increased from 12% to 16%.

However, the company has huge debts (approximately £1.2 billion), which were used to finance the buyout in 2003. This creates a risk for managers if interest rates increase or sales fall. Debenhams has also sold all of its prime properties, which helped to finance some of the £1.3 billion paid out in dividends to its new shareholders. In the last $2\frac{1}{2}$ years, it has also cut back on capital spending, investing less on improving its stores than the smaller John Lewis spent in 1 year alone.

In contrast, Marks and Spencer has focused less on changing finances and has looked instead at its retailing activities — for example, cutting costs and winning customers. The company has improved its new lines and reduced prices (its prices used to be about 4% higher than those at Debenhams, but they are now 10% lower than 3 years ago). Its net profit margin has fallen from 10% to around 8% over the same period.

Q13.2 Which business (M&S or Debenhams) do you think is in a stronger long-term position?

Vodafone

For over 20 years, Vodafone (a wireless telecommunications company) has aimed to:
- go global to achieve economies of scale
- be involved in mobile technology, focusing on the wireless segment of the market rather than landlines

On 30 May 2006, after years of success, Vodafone announced a loss of £22 billion — the largest loss in European company history. This was attributed to 'write-offs' caused by paying too much for various acquisitions. When the acquisitions proved to be worth less than was paid for them, the accounts needed to be changed. The company cut between £23 billion and £28 billion from the £81.5 billion of goodwill listed on its balance sheet. Most of this was goodwill incurred when it bought Mannesmann in Germany for £101 billion at the height of the telecoms boom in 2000.

This announcement came on top of other criticism of Vodafone's strategy, on the basis that:
- the focus on scale may have achieved some economies of scale, but it does not mean that the bigger company was run efficiently overall
- its focus may have been too narrow, given that technological developments have allowed its rivals to offer broadband and television services

Vodafone is now trying to change its strategy. First, in March 2006, it sold its Japanese subsidiary (J-Phone, bought in 2001) and may soon sell some more of its companies. Second, the firm is trying to broaden its range by working with partners to offer broadband access and allow instant messaging to be used on mobile phones.

The announcement of Vodafone's write-offs caused some investors to question the management of the company, in particular the role of Arun Sarin, the company's chief executive. At the company's annual general meeting in 2006, 15% of its investors voted against Sarin's re-election or abstained.

Q13.3 Should the chief executive always be held responsible for the poor performance of a company?

Nationwide and Portman proposed merger

The Nationwide and Portman building societies announced in 2006 that they would merge, creating the UK's second largest mortgage lender. The new company (to be called Nationwide) will have more than 800 branches across the UK and more than 13 million members in total. Nationwide is the UK's largest building society, while Portman is the third biggest. The motive behind the deal is 'synergy', i.e. the benefits that combined businesses get by sharing resources and skills, making them stronger than when operating individually. The bigger company would be able to borrow money at a cheaper rate and make cost savings (e.g. by avoiding duplication of resources). The deal is expected to be completed by September 2007.

Q13.4 Why do governments sometimes act to prevent mergers?

Piaggio turnaround

In 2003, the IMMSI group bought a controlling stake in the scooter business Piaggio. At that time, Piaggio had large debts that were swallowing its earnings. The company was established originally to make bomber aeroplanes before it moved into scooter manufacture. Its most famous brand, the Vespa, is now 60 years old, but in 2003 sales were low and the business struggled against rivals such as Honda and Yamaha. The company also had poor relations with its workforce and lost 48,600 hours of work to strikes in 2003. Losses in that year reached £94 million. By 2006, the company had been turned around quite dramatically.

The new owners focused on reducing the debt, developing new models, boosting quality and improving relations with staff. They also aimed to produce higher volumes in order to benefit from economies of scale. This was achieved by moving into motorbikes and investing heavily in research and development. The turnaround began by switching debt for shares in the company in order to reduce interest payments. Next came investment to improve working conditions, in particular introducing air conditioning to make the temperature more tolerable for employees at the Piaggio factory. Employees were guaranteed their jobs and given more flexible contracts. Investment in machinery improved quality, and refurbished buildings increased the flow of work. Cheaper components were found in China and India, leading to major cost savings.

Piaggio also bought Aprilia, a producer of high-powered bikes that was close to bankruptcy. This acquisition permitted economies of scale in engine development. Rechargeable hybrid engine models have also been developed to meet current consumer demands. The company is now working on more products: for example, in India it is selling a three-wheeled scooter for use as a light cargo vehicle and rickshaw.

Eddie Stobart diversifies

Eddie Stobart, the UK's largest privately owned haulage business and one of Cumbria's most famous companies, announced in 2006 that it was investigating new business areas. The company prides itself on its smartly dressed drivers and high-profile brand name and colours. The brand is so well known that there is even an Eddie Stobart fan club, with a range of toys and clothes. In 2001, when the haulage business suffered because of high petrol prices, the company made more profit from the fan club than from its core business.

In 2003, the family business was bought by a railway infrastructure company, WA Developments, but a member of the Stobart family is still chief executive. The new owners helped to turn the business around and its customers now include Coca-Cola, Sara Lee and Tesco. The company is now exploring new methods of transporting goods, as shown by its recent move into rail freight. An interest in air freight has influenced the location of its new headquarters, which are to be built at Carlisle Airport (bought by the company in 2005). Eddie Stobart plans to make Carlisle a major regional airport, with flights to the south of England as well as Europe.

Q13.6 Why might Eddie Stobart have chosen this moment to expand into other areas of distribution?

Ford to cut costs

In January 2006, Ford announced factory closures to cut production capacity in the USA, because of its falling share in the US market. Ford's plans include the closure of several assembly plants and the loss of up to 30,000 jobs. Most of the redundancies are factory jobs, but some management positions will also be lost. These changes are part of Ford's latest plan, called 'The Way Forward'.

Ford has been hit hard by rising imports and the increasing costs of pensions and healthcare. The situation was made worse by problems in its European division and by losses at Jaguar. Ford's automotive losses in the first 9 months of 2005 were $1.7 billion. Its only profit comes from lending customers the money to buy its cars through its credit division.

To bring about real change, Ford needs the cooperation of the trade unions, which are powerful in its US factories. Any job losses need to be carefully negotiated with the United Auto Workers (UAW) union and deals will need to be made if Ford is to become profitable again.

To lead the change, the company hired Alan Mulally in September 2006 as chief executive. Mulally had previously worked at Boeing. He took over from

William Ford Junior, the great-grandson of Ford's founder, Henry Ford. Ford Junior had been unable to make the business work, whereas Mulally had successfully turned around Boeing. At the aeroplane manufacturer, Mulally made thousands of workers redundant and introduced lean production into plane manufacturing. However, success in the automotive industry is not just about producing cars efficiently. It also involves getting consumers to buy the products. Unfortunately, Ford's product portfolio is perceived to be dull and the company has been losing sales steadily to rivals such as Toyota.

Q13.7 What could Ford do to improve its performance?

Chapter 14

Business ethics

About this chapter

The term 'business ethics' refers to what managers believe is the right or wrong decision for a company. How important is it to pay suppliers on time? To what extent should a firm offer employees a career rather than just a job? Should a business try to recruit local staff? These are all ethical issues.

The Body Shop is closely associated with ethics — especially animal rights and environmental protection. Driven by the passion and beliefs of its founder, Anita Roddick, The Body Shop has led the way on many causes. In 2006, L'Oréal, a multinational cosmetics firm, took over The Body Shop, thus combining two very different companies. It will be interesting to watch the progress of this new business.

It is often assumed that younger people have a keen interest in environmental and ethical issues. However, a survey in 2006 revealed that shoppers under 25 have less interest in ethical issues than older buyers. Nevertheless, environmental issues are clearly important to many consumers, investors and employees. Therefore, it is not surprising that organisations are trying to reduce the negative impact of their activities on the environment. In 2006, the main supermarkets announced the steps that they are taking to reduce environmental damage.

Ethical business?

In 2006, L'Oréal made a successful takeover bid for The Body Shop. While The Body Shop had built its reputation on being socially responsible, L'Oréal was better known for its high-profile materialistic values and its focus on beauty — 'because you're worth it'. This is one of the latest in a series of deals in which big firms have bought smaller companies that have a reputation for social responsibility:

- In 2000, Unilever bought Ben & Jerry's, a US icecream maker with a strong sense of social responsibility.
- In 2001, McDonald's bought a 33% share of Pret A Manger, a London-based chain of sandwich shops, committed to 'no additives, no preservatives'.
- In 2005, Cadbury Schweppes bought Green & Black's, a chocolate maker devoted to organic ingredients and 362 'ethical values'.

L'Oréal has stated that The Body Shop will be allowed to operate as an independent business, but only time will tell whether L'Oréal's products start to appear in The Body Shop stores.

Q14.1 Why might large multinational firms such as L'Oréal want to be associated with ethical firms such as The Body Shop?

Do we care?

According to a survey in 2006, over half of shoppers aged under 25 do not care how their clothes are produced. This suggests that organisations promoting fair trade goods, organic cotton and ethically produced products still have much work to do to. Less than 30% of shoppers said that they would be willing to pay more money to guarantee that their clothes had been produced sustainably. Younger buyers are less interested in these issues than their parents and grandparents. Over one-third of consumers aged over 55 would look at the label to find out the country of origin before deciding whether to buy; for under-25s, the proportion was 9%. The key ethical issue was child labour, which was regarded as much more important than the use of organic fabric.

Marks and Spencer was judged to be the most ethical retailer of 2006, according to Business in the Community, with a rating of 3.27 (on a scale from 1 to 5). The company launched a fair trade cotton clothing range, as part of its 'Look Behind the Label' campaign, which aims to inform shoppers about where its products come from.

Q14.2 Should retailers stock 'ethical' products?

Supermarkets go green

Sainsbury's announced that it will sell over 500 of its own-brand products in packaging that can be composted (i.e. not plastic) in an attempt to be more environmentally friendly. It is claimed this would save over 3,500 tonnes of plastic a year. The company said that it wanted others to follow its lead and encouraged the government to provide compost bins for households. Tesco adopted a different strategy to prove its environmental credentials and launched an advertising campaign to encourage people to re-use plastic carrier bags with the incentive of extra customer loyalty points.

Environmental campaigners responded positively to the innovations at Tesco and Sainsbury's, but they stressed that this is only the start. For example, Friends of the Earth said that local shops and markets are often more environmentally sound as they source local produce and sell fresh goods without unnecessary packaging. Another pressure group, called WasteWatch, said that its aim was to persuade supermarkets to sell more food such as fruit without any packaging. Others groups pointed out that there is still much to be done. Although Sainsbury's initiative for compostable packaging covers 500 lines, a typical supermarket can have 40,000 different products.

Soon after Sainsbury's move, Wal-Mart announced that it was going to reduce packaging by 5% over 5 years. The scheme will start in 2008 and should save around $3.4 billion (£1.78 billion), as well as preventing 'millions of pounds of trash reaching landfills'.

Q14.3 Should Sainsbury's make the packaging of all its products more environmentally friendly?

Chapter 15

Business trends

About this chapter

A notable business trend in 2006 was the continued rise in foreign takeovers of UK firms. Another involved private investment companies buying public companies and making them private in order to turn them around. A third trend was increased social philanthropy — when business people give large sums of money to good causes. This has raised interesting questions about the role of business in society and the extent to which it is a force for good. There was also a rise in the number of start-ups in the UK — an important development, as new firms provide innovation and employment, as well as competition for established firms. Of course, it is not just how many firms start up that matters — what is also important is how long they last and how successful they become, and this depends on many internal and external factors.

Overseas takeovers

For many years before 2004, UK firms spent more on buying companies abroad than foreign firms spent to acquire UK businesses. For example, between 1996 and 2003, UK firms spent £469 billion on buying overseas companies; foreign acquisitions in the UK were worth only £234 billion. In 2004, the situation began to change: spending on companies in the UK was £29.9 billion, compared with £18.6 billion of UK spending abroad. In 2005, UK companies spent £32.7 billion in 365 transactions to purchase overseas companies. This was clearly outweighed by £50.3 billion paid by foreign firms to acquire UK businesses. This trend continued in 2006 (see Table 15.1).

UK firm	Purchaser	Country	Value of deal (£m)
O_2	Telefónica	Spain	17,610
BAA	Ferrovial	Spain	15,656
BOC Group	Linde	Germany	8,919
P&O	Dubai Ports World	Dubai	4,565
BPB	Saint-Gobain	France	4,389
Exel	Deutsche Post	Germany	4,032
Hilton International	Hilton Hotels Corporation	USA	3,298
Pilkington	Nippon Sheet Glass	Japan	2,433

Source: Mergermarket, *Sunday Times*, 25 June 2006

Table 15.1 Examples of UK companies bought by foreign firms in 2006

The private equity boom

In recent years, private equity takeovers have played an important part in UK business. Private equity firms are made up of private investors that take over a company and work closely with the managers to turn the business around. Their aim is to make it profitable and then sell it. Therefore, they look for businesses that are undervalued and can be improved. Private equity firms often buy public limited companies, make them private, improve them and then sell them back to the public. When public limited companies are listed on the Stock Exchange, managers often find that the investors are interested only in short-term rewards. This can make it difficult to invest in longer-term projects or to take risks in decision making. Radical, daring or innovative decisions may be shelved in favour of conservative and potentially uninspiring choices.

Reporting to many different investors takes up a lot of management time. When a private equity company takes over a public limited company, it empowers the managers to run the business and make the right decisions, even if they are high risk or take years to pay off. The private equity firm is closely involved in the running of the business and in developing the right strategy. However, such takeovers are usually financed by debt, so they are high risk. Some private equity firms have been accused of being asset strippers — buying a company to squeeze out whatever profits they can get before selling it on.

Private equity firms have made bids for many well-known UK companies, such as Gala, Vodafone Japan, House of Fraser, HMV, ITV, Associated British Ports, Kwik-Fit, Debenhams, Somerfield, Halfords and the AA. Not all of these bids are successful. Some shareholders assume that a bid from a private equity company means that a business is undervalued, so they are reluctant to sell. For example, in 2006, Permira's £843-million offer for music retailer HMV and the Apax consortium's £1.5-billion offer for ITV were both rejected.

Social responsibility: social philanthropy

In 2006, several prominent businesspeople donated large sums of money to good causes (known as 'social philanthropy'). For example, Warren Buffett, a leading US investor, pledged to give most of his $44-billion fortune to the charitable foundation established by Bill Gates, the founder of Microsoft. Earlier in the year Bill Gates announced that he was stepping down from Microsoft to work full time at the foundation with his wife. Buffett has already given around $31 billion to the foundation. His donation makes the Gates Foundation the world's biggest charitable organisation. It has overtaken the

Stichting INGKA Foundation, which owns the Swedish furniture company IKEA. Table 15.2 lists some of business's top philanthropists.

	Sum donated
Carnegie	$350 million
Rockefeller	$450 million
Gates	$35 billion
Buffett	$31 billion

Source: BEA, Datapedia

Table 15.2 Top philanthropists

In 2006, Sir Richard Branson revealed that he will invest $3 billion (around £1.6 billion) to fight global warming. Branson said that he will give up all the profits from his travel firms (including Virgin Atlantic and Virgin Trains) for the next 10 years. The money will be invested in renewable energy technologies through a fund called Virgin Fuels.

Social philanthropy is not new. In the UK, Joseph Rowntree, the founder of the confectionery business, set up several trusts in the nineteenth century, pursuing his religious Quaker ideals of social improvement. The Leverhulme Trust was established by the Lever brothers and is now worth more than £1 billion. The Sainsbury family has 19 family trusts that donate money to the arts, education, research and healthcare. The Esmée Fairbairn Foundation was created in 1961 by the founder of the M&G unit trust group in memory of his wife. It has assets worth more than £800 million and makes grants to improve the quality of life of UK citizens. In 2005, the Scottish entrepreneur Sir Tom Hunter gave former US president Bill Clinton's Global Initiative £100 million to fight world poverty and to be spent on health, education, agriculture and entrepreneurial support in Malawi and Rwanda. The *Sunday Times* Giving Index showed that in 2006 the top 30 philanthropists increased their donations from £333 million in 2005 to £453 million. However, the level of charitable giving in the UK is 0.84% of GDP — much less than the 1.85% donated in the USA.

Q15.3 Do you think that profitable businesses should donate some of their money to charitable organisations?

Start-ups and entrepreneurs

Figures released by Barclays Bank in 2006 showed a substantial increase in the number of entrepreneurs. Estimates show that 110,300 new businesses started up in the first quarter of 2006 — almost one quarter more than in the same period in 2005 (88,800). Other interesting findings include the following:

- 20,600 women started a business in the first quarter of 2006 compared with 16,700 for the same period the year before. (The number of men setting up a business in the first quarter of 2006 was 75,400.)
- Property services showed the biggest percentage growth.

At the same time, there was an increase in the volume of business closures. In the first quarter of 2006, 111,200 companies ceased trading — an increase of nearly 50% compared with the same period in 2005. However, because there are more businesses operating, as a percentage of the total number of firms this figure has remained constant for the last 10 years.

Q15.4 Why do more men than women set up new businesses? Why do so many firms close down?

Chapter 16

The UK today

About this chapter

It can be fascinating to look at the key business features of different countries. Questions you can ask include:

- what is the standard of living?
- who owns what?
- how open is the country to trade?
- what proportion of the economy is in the primary, secondary or tertiary sectors?
- how do people use their time?

Analysing this information helps organisations to identify opportunities in a market and to evaluate their own business strategies. An enormous amount of secondary data is available in newspapers, on the internet and via government sources (e.g. the Office for National Statistics, www.ons.gov.uk). This chapter presents a snapshot of various aspects of the UK, such as share ownership, population data and ownership of consumer goods. This sort of information provides an interesting insight and is a useful starting point for many market-led organisations.

Share ownership

Figure 16.1 illustrates how the ownership of the UK's public limited companies is distributed.

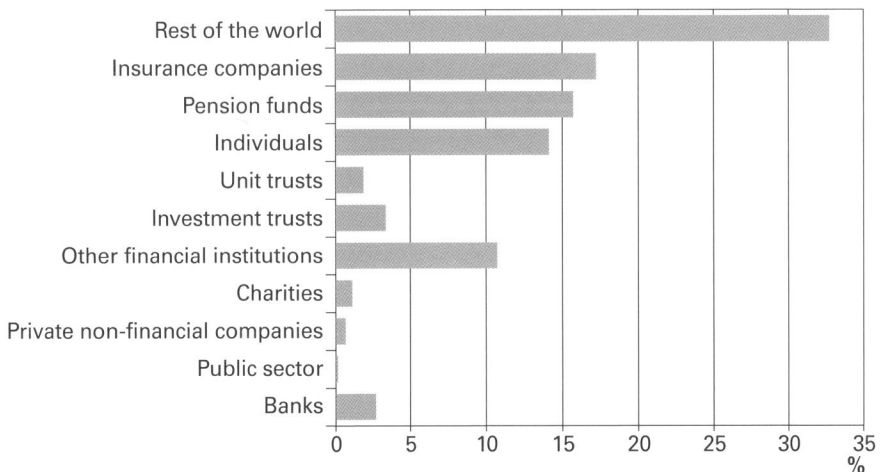

Source: Office for National Statistics

Figure 16.1 Distribution of ownership of the UK's public limited companies

Key points include the following:
- Overseas investors own 33% of UK shares listed on the London Stock Exchange.
- Private individuals hold around 14% of these companies' shares.
- Almost 50% of all ordinary shares listed on the UK Stock Exchange are held by insurance companies, pension funds and other institutional shareholders.

Q16.1 How might the fact that over 50% of ordinary shares are held by insurance companies, pension funds and other institutional share-holders affect the objectives of UK companies on the Stock Exchange?

Population

Over the last 30 years, the UK population has been ageing. In the total population of almost 60 million (Table 16.1), around 16% are aged over 65 (Figure 16.2). The proportion under 16 is around 19%. This changes consumption patterns in the UK and also creates opportunities and threats in the labour market for UK firms.

Region	Population	Proportion of total UK population (%)
England	50,093,100	83.7
Scotland	5,078,400	8.5
Wales	2,952,500	4.9
Northern Ireland	1,710,300	2.9
UK	**59,834,300**	**100.0**

Table 16.1 UK population by region

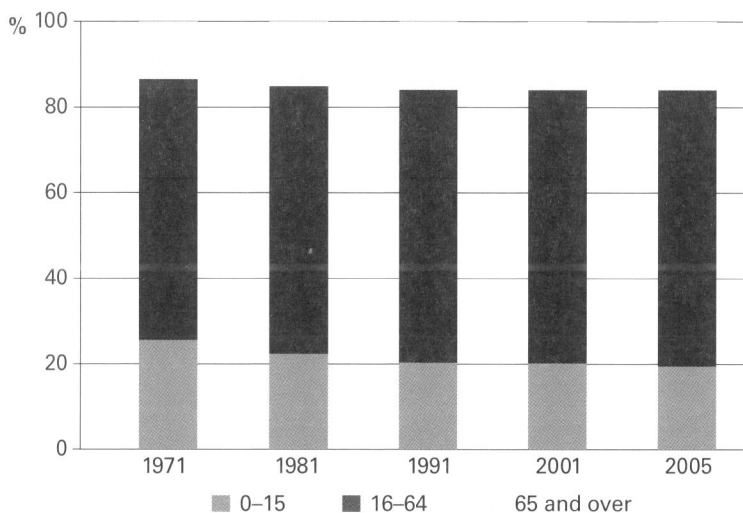

Figure 16.2 Distribution of age ranges in the UK population, 1971–2005

Q16.2 Why do you think that the population is ageing? Is this important to business?

UK households

Information on UK households is gathered every 10 years through a national census. The last census in the UK was 2001. This showed that there were 21,660,475 households in England and Wales.

Single-person households
30.0% of households in the UK consist of only one person. This is an increase from the 1991 value of 26.3%. Nearly half of the one-person households (3.1 million) are one-pensioner households and three-quarters of these (2,366,000) are occupied by a woman living on her own. Single-person households are least likely to have amenities such as central heating or sole use of a bath/shower and toilet. More than one in eight of single-person households do not have central heating.

Ownership of consumer goods
Figure 16.3 illustrates the proportion of UK households that have various consumer goods.

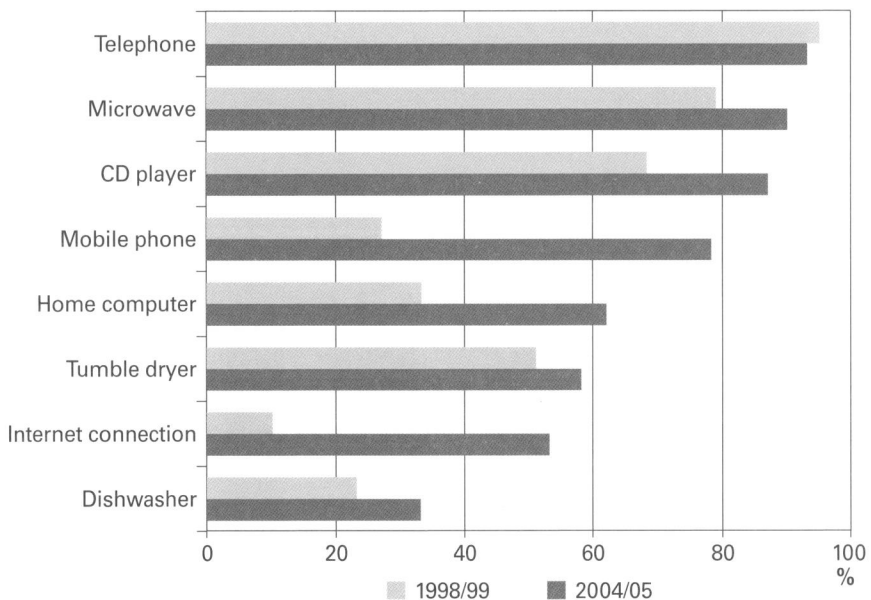

Source: Office for National Statistics

Figure 16.3 Ownership of consumer goods by the UK population, 1998–2005

- Between 1998/99 and 2004/05, the proportion of UK households with a home computer increased from 33% to 62%; internet connections also increased — from 9% to 53%.

- The percentage of households that own a dishwasher, tumble dryer and microwave grew to 33%, 58% and 90% respectively in 2004/05.
- There was also a considerable increase after 1998/99 in the proportion of households with a mobile phone (from 27% to 78%).
- In 2004/05, most homes had central heating (95%) and a washing machine (95%).

How people in the UK use their time

Table 16.2 shows how people aged 16 and above in the UK use their time.

	Hours and minutes per day	
	Males over 15	Females over 15
Sleep	8.04	8.18
Resting	0.43	0.48
Personal care	0.40	0.48
Eating/drinking	1.25	1.19
Leisure		
Watching television/videos/DVDs and listening to radio/music	2.50	2.25
Social life and entertainment/culture	1.22	1.32
Hobbies and games	0.37	0.23
Sport	0.13	0.07
Reading	0.23	0.26
All leisure	5.25	4.53
Employment and study	3.45	2.26
Housework	1.41	3.00
Childcare	0.15	0.32
Voluntary work and meetings	0.15	0.20
Travel	1.32	1.22
Other	0.13	0.15

Source: Office for National Statistics

Table 16.2 Time allocated to daily activities, 2005

People in the UK spend most of their time on three main activities: sleeping, working and watching television/videos/DVDs or listening to the radio/music. These activities take up over half the day (on average 13 hours and 38 minutes). About one third of the day is spent sleeping. Men are more likely to watch television or listen to the radio and to take part in activities such as sport, hobbies and using the computer. Women are more likely than men to read or to spend time with other people.

The distribution of activities varies during the week. At the weekend, both men and women spend more time sleeping and participating in leisure activities;

men also spent more time on domestic work (161 minutes, compared with 116 minutes on weekdays).

Q16.3 How might the data in Table 16.2 be useful to UK firms?

UK spending

A report published in 2006 noted that consumer spending in the UK reached a record £1,000,000,000,000. The biggest area of spending is housing (about £327 billion). However, the largest growth areas are items such as cars, DVD players, luxury furniture and holidays. The annual *British Lifestyles* report by the consumer-spending analyst Mintel showed the following:

- The average household spends £37,000 a year on consumer goods. Priority items include satellite navigation systems, flat-screen televisions and holidays.
- The cost of holidays has reached an average of £790 a year for every adult and child in the UK.
- Spending in the home-appliance market has moved away from 'white goods' (e.g. fridges, dishwashers, freezers) to 'brown goods' (e.g. televisions, DVD players, stereos).
- Spending on home computers has been growing rapidly, despite falling prices.
- Spending on occasional items that are neither essential nor luxury (e.g. books, gym memberships, visits to the cinema) accounts for 16% of the consumer market. Particularly popular are hair and beauty treatments, household goods and gadgets, and plants and flowers.

Q16.4 How might information on consumer spending be valuable to UK firms?

Answer notes

Chapter 1

Q1.1 Entrance of new competitors; managing growth (e.g. controlling a larger operation); change in trends/tastes; slower growth once people have bought the product.

Q1.2 'Can-do' culture means people feel empowered and sense that goals can be achieved; can be developed by delegating, giving people expectations, celebrating success.

Q1.3 Less interference from outside investors; lower public profile; less regulation; less vulnerable to takeover.

Q1.4 Has tapped into a fast-growing market, has good technology and promoted itself well, possibly by word of mouth; big pay-outs may be attractive and nature of the games may be appealing.

Q1.5 Better attendance; better productivity; people may stay longer; more cooperation; greater willingness to put forward ideas.

Q1.6 May lead to a better image and therefore make it easier to attract investors, employees and customers; might be mutually beneficial (e.g. better conditions for employees may mean greater productivity); investment in the community could mean more favourable treatment from local council.

Q1.7 Good for environment; may attract consumers, employees and investors; might be the 'right' thing to do, but could mean lower output and reduced sales; depends on relative costs and benefits, environmental stance of directors and legislation.

Q1.8 Nonrestrictive legislation; tax system that favours business; English is worldwide language; government subsidies; uncorrupt system; member of European Union.

Q1.9 Funds may be more readily available for expansion. Because the USA is a big market, it can expand domestically and gain economies of scale. Based on this, it can then expand further and be competitive. This competitiveness within the USA may lead to greater efficiency, enabling successful overseas expansion.

Q1.10 More interest in environmental issues; increased number of cycle lanes; higher car taxes.

Chapter 2

Q2.1 Probably unavoidable, but can learn from fraud cases and develop new legislation and new practices (e.g. more outsiders on boards of directors, ethical committees, immunity for whistleblowers).

Q2.2 Success will depend on quality of services and size of market; also on whether competitors come into the market and how well the business is run.

Q2.3 Chairman oversees the actions of the managers, including the chief executive. If the roles are combined, the chief executive is monitoring and supervising his/her own work; could be dangerous and remove a valuable check on a chief executive's actions.

Q2.4 Conflict of interest: auditors may not want to look for problems in case they lose contract; may be more eager to please those who are paying bill than serve public interest.

Q2.5 Person who does not have a daily job in the business; non-executive directors do not have 'executive' power internally (i.e. they are from outside the firm); may bring with them experience from other organisations and offer objective views of the business.

Chapter 3

Q3.1 Lack of demand; viewing figures too low to justify investment; may be because of many other ways of accessing music today and/or because it was seen as a tired brand.

Q3.2 May be worried about backlash from media and parents; public opinion has changed, so many firms see this form of marketing as unethical; some organisations want to do (or be seen to be doing) right thing.

Q3.3 Change in customer tastes; many of its products might have seemed old-fashioned; children mature at younger ages; less demand for this type of entertainment; more alternatives available.

Q3.4 Depends on number of potential buyers and perceived value to them. What assets does the business have? Can the brand be extended on to other products? What is the likely demand for such a luxury car? How desperate is Ford to sell? May want to sell now because it needs the money; thinks it will get a good price; is changing its strategy and Aston Martin no longer fits with this; may have recent problems (e.g. employer/employee relations).

Q3.5 Company could try to lobby government (e.g. through members of parliament); could try to generate press interest or alter product (e.g. make it slower).

Chapter 4

Q4.1 More interest in healthy food; more concern over diet; higher standards of living; greater supply and greater availability in stores; better labelling.

Q4.2 Actions of competitors; product itself (e.g. taste); market needs and demands (e.g. for sugar-free products); extent and effectiveness of promotion.

Q4.3 Could change its promotional message (e.g. good for brain, instead of fun and exciting); change distribution (e.g. find new outlets); alter product (e.g. mind games rather than action games); pricing may reflect benefits to user (e.g. worth paying a lot to improve your memory).

Q4.4 Product has been changed (e.g. new outfits, friends, equipment, interests, activities); targeting new countries; developing new promotional campaigns.

Q4.5 Increased demand for small size (e.g. growth of laptop market and decline of desktop); consumers want more computing power but greater ease of accessing this and carrying it around with them; more demand to be online, to access film and video, to use computers to control more devices (e.g. within home).

Q4.6 Likely to increase overheads; if demand not there to support increased capacity in long term, could lead to losses; high risk.

Q4.7 Decision may be justified because of supermarket's previous treatment of company; may have genuine ethical concerns; may want to protect exclusivity of brand; may want more control over where and how it is distributed; may have a deal with Waitrose; controversy also generates publicity.

Q4.8 Using past experience of its own promotions and/or those of other firms; best guess of experts; extrapolating from test market.

Q4.9 Brand name is an asset; may bring customer loyalty; saves money on building new brand; may be easier to launch new products under established brand name.

Q4.10 Likely demand; fit with skills and assets of business; what product range to stock; what level of service to provide; how to brand; what price range to target.

Chapter 5

Q5.1 For B&Q, better cashflow; for suppliers, cashflow problems, which could affect companies' survival and jobs; clearly associated ethical issues; action may adversely affect brand image of B&Q.

Q5.2 Company has generated large amount of money, but would need to consider issues such as size of business and therefore rate of return; also need to take into account profit trends and competitors' profits. Is this level of profit sustainable? To what extent is the firm achieving immediate profits at the expense of long-term investment?

Q5.3 Unlikely to be possible to prevent fraud completely; can be reduced by better legislation, better inspection procedures and safeguards, more trials; there will always be some attempts to defraud investors.

Chapter 6

Q6.1 Allows company to attract more/better applicants for job; keep employees for longer, thus reducing recruitment and induction training costs.

Q6.2 Companies may have to pay higher wages in order to recruit staff; may have to work harder to retain employees; may not be able to meet work targets if cannot get staff.

Q6.3 Power determined by number of members, how well organised they are, legal situation (e.g. protest rights), availability of alternative sources of labour, impact of industrial action on a firm.

Q6.4 Depends on whether this was the only communication; if this was a typical style (i.e. part of culture); whether the sender is perceived as important and has power; what action follows it.

Q6.5 High pay levels may be justified on basis of profits earned and the employees' contribution to success of business. But can they be justified in view of average wages in the country/levels of inequality?

Q6.6 Need for minimum wage depends on how firms would act without such a law; may be pressure to cut costs and therefore pay low wages; would firms see benefits of paying a 'reasonable' wage without legislation?

Chapter 7

Q7.1 Airbus may lose business; have to pay penalties; be so focused on getting existing products right that it cannot work on long-term development of other planes; make a loss and be vulnerable to takeover.

Q7.2 Depends on how many faults and how serious they are. What would be the impact on customer goodwill and loyalty? What are the benefits of getting the product to the market earlier rather than later?

Q7.3 Recall could lead to loss of goodwill; could damage brand values; could hit sales of other Cadbury products and make new launches more difficult; might reduce profits.

Q7.4 Ease of coordinating and managing operations at different locations; ease of recruitment; impact on brand image; availability and quality of suppliers; government incentives.

Chapter 8

Q8.1 Apple can continue to innovate and build brand, but technology can probably be imitated; customers become more concerned with price than design; may depend on Apple's ability to stay ahead of the market.

Q8.2 Collusion can help fix prices and increase profits; OFT would investigate to find out whether consumers are being exploited and whether companies are acting 'against the public interest'.

Q8.3 Guaranteed immunity may encourage people to come forward and therefore act as deterrent to prevent other cartels from forming; may depend on how involved company is in collusion.

Chapter 9

Q9.1 Value of brand; perceived brand image; income levels abroad; foreign competition abroad; exchange rate; any protectionist controls.

Q9.2 Expansion provides more opportunities for sales; in UK, increasing criticism of Tesco's power, so overseas expansion helps avoid further criticism at home; USA is big market; consumers speak English; close US and UK links, which may make it easier to operate there and understand the culture; may be gap in US market for Tesco's type of local convenience store.

Q9.3 Just because it has been unsuccessful in some markets does not mean that all overseas expansions will fail; international markets provide opportunity for expansion that may be necessary for continued growth; may need to plan better and choose country more carefully, but unlikely to stop overseas expansion.

Chapter 10

Q10.1 Huge potential profits available in this fast-growing market, but recent arrests suggest USA legislation may limit success; might be better to wait for outcome of court cases; however, even with US opposition, unlikely that these markets will disappear.

Q10.2 Sends signal that car companies need to think hard about environmental impact of their actions (e.g. greater consideration of fuel efficiency).

Q10.3 Consumer trends (e.g. growing interest in health and concern over fizzy, sugary drinks); actions of other producers and of retailers; effectiveness of marketing strategies; perception abroad of US producers (e.g. anti-American protests).

Chapter 11

Q11.1 Many mobile phone owners and strong interest in film and television programmes; mobile phones could provide easy, convenient way of watching such programmes; depends on quality of screen and content, as well as price.

Q11.2 To enable fast growth; to block competitors; perceives a high return as it can apply its advertising model and technological skills; cannot see its own site achieving these viewing figures.

Q11.3 Offers customers greater convenience, which adds value; could be cheaper and save time; may not have been launched before because of technological problems (e.g. security issues).

Chapter 12

Q12.1   Products that may experience increased demand include takeways, canned drinks, home-delivery foods, boxes of chocolate and popcorn; restaurants, cinemas and theatres may suffer fall in demand.

Q12.2   Television companies may get more viewers and be able to charge advertisers higher prices (during prolonged bad weather); other businesses that may benefit include makers of raincoats, umbrellas and hot drinks, and book retailers.

Q12.3   GDP growth figures may be useful for estimating likely growth in demand for some products (e.g. income-elastic versus income-inelastic); may give insight into rise in standard of living, from which to predict changes in consumption patterns; inflation data may affect competitiveness of firms in particular country; can make deductions about likely government policy (e.g. interest rate changes) and how it will affect a business.

Q12.4   Examples of such global products include cigarettes, jeans, trainers, watches, sunglasses.

Q12.5   Increased costs and increased uncertainty, which act as deterrent for investment; may be difficult to export as products will be comparatively expensive.

Q12.6   High interest rates may lead to lower borrowing, thus reducing demand; in turn, this may reduce demand-pull inflation.

Q12.7   Good for firms involved in education sector (e.g. builders of schools, textbook publishers, school-equipment producers); tax on alcohol and tobacco may lead to healthier workforce and less absenteeism/sickness; higher tax allowances may leave people with more income and so boost spending (e.g. on consumer goods); similarly, higher pay may encourage more spending, thus increasing demand for some firms; economic growth may encourage investment and expansion, benefiting producers of industrial equipment.

Q12.8   House prices increase usually because of increasing demand relative to supply; in housing shortage, house prices increase.

Q12.9   Higher oil prices increase costs for firms, which can reduce profits; some projects may become unviable; this may reduce investment and economic growth.

Q12.10 In order to maintain innovation and economic growth; may increase number of new products and processes.

Q12.11 Greater tax on air travel; tax on miles travelled, pollution or refuse.

Chapter 13

Q13.1   Depends on costs, what competitors are doing, target market, what alternatives there are (opportunity costs), which retail outlets are used.

Q13.2 More likely to be M&S on basis of information given — owns own stores, so has a lot of collateral; does not have huge debts; seems to have improved product portfolio and become more efficient; seems to have adopted major change in approach; Debenhams may be getting more out of its assets, but not building as much for future.

Q13.3 Ultimately, chief executive has to be accountable for performance of business, although may be many external factors that influence success or failure of organisation.

Q13.4 Because mergers can lead to monopoly power, less choice and higher prices for consumers, exploitation.

Q13.5 Economies of scale bring down unit costs, making the firm more competitive with rivals; products can then be offered at low prices for mass market; probably a competitive market, so firms are up against low-cost producers — important to be as efficient as possible.

Q13.6 Company may have resources to expand now; may be worried about future taxation policies and pressure affecting road-haulage industry; may want to offer broader service; may have seized an opportunity (e.g. to buy Carlisle airport).

Q13.7 Improve its product portfolio (will take time); improve quality and reduce costs; develop clearer vision and stronger leadership.

Chapter 14

Q14.1 Ethical firms have good reputation and positive association in consumers' and investors' minds; may protect against adverse publicity and pressure group action; may offer opportunities for growth.

Q14.2 Yes, if retailers believe that it is right to stock such products and that they will appeal to certain sections of the market; however, demand may not necessarily be great.

Q14.3 Depends on cost, values of the directors and owners, relative impact on environment, priorities for business.

Chapter 15

Q15.1 UK company accounts readily available and reveal much information under UK accounting regulations, so potential buyers know what they are getting; the UK media and government not against foreign takeovers, so foreign buyer is likely to be able to go ahead without huge opposition; UK shareholders often have short-term outlooks and are willing to sell if offer is right; UK shares spread more widely among shareholders and these investors seem less loyal to existing managers (in countries such as Spain and Germany, shareholder structure offers protection against takeovers; families and institutions often hold large proportions of shares and block takeovers); UK firms relatively cheap;

UK share prices typically equal to 13 times the profits (for European firms this is often 14 times, so shares more expensive to buy).

Q15.2 Provides access to many more investors and has greater status; likely to lead to greater media attention, but can be expensive to float business; more vulnerable to takeover.

Q15.3 Depends on owners' wishes, how much money and the recipients.

Q15.4 May be due to social conditioning; men may have more role models than women; many firms close because of lack of planning, poor business training, lack of government support, actions of bigger firms, problems coordinating all different aspects of business.

Chapter 16

Q16.1 May put pressure on firms to deliver short-term results; this may deter managers from making long-term investments, developing short-term outlook.

Q16.2 Lower birth rates and people living longer (e.g. because of better diets and medical care); leads to change in consumption patterns; different human resource policies needed to attract and keep older workers; may need to change retirement policies, reduce age discrimination and consider pension plans.

Q16.3 Data give insight into UK life and highlight business opportunities for firms; how consumers spend their time might prompt development of new products to fit these habits.

Q16.4 Marketing opportunities may follow from information on which products households have/do not have; information on access to internet and mobile phones may lead to possible media ventures.

2006 quiz

Below is a list of 50 questions that test how much you have learnt about what happened in the world of business in 2006. All the answers are contained in Chapters 1–16.

1   Which firm bought The Body Shop?

2   Whom did Ford hire to turn the company around? For which company did he work before joining Ford?

3   Name three of the top CoolBrands.

4   Which firm bought O_2? Name a UK company that was bought by an overseas buyer.

5   Which supermarket announced that it was using more environmentally friendly packaging for many of its product lines?

6   Which road-haulage company decided to expand into rail freight?

7   What was the average house price in the UK?

8   Which organisation increased interest rates in the UK?

9   Which country experienced an inflation rate over 1,000%?

10   Which supermarket chain withdrew from Germany?

11   Which supermarket chain announced its entry into the US market?

12   Which company was *The Times* Employer of the Year?

13   Which company put Aston Martin up for sale?

14   Which computer manufacturer considered selling through retail outlets for the first time?

15   Which oil company reported the largest corporate profits in the UK?

16   Which music television programme was taken off the air after 40 years?

17   Which model maker hit financial problems?

18   Which major football sporting event affected some firms enormously?

19   Which firm bought the company that created the Crazy Frog ringtone?

20 Which airline was accused of colluding over prices?

21 Name a teenage magazine that was closed down.

22 Which everyday item can now be bought online and printed direct onto envelopes?

23 Which supermarket MD announced that he was standing down to become chairman only?

24 Marks and Spencer announced the future launch of which type of products?

25 Which manufacturer reported delays with its A380 aircraft?

26 The corporate fraud trial of which company began in Italy?

27 Which firm bought the Rover brand name?

28 Which cider company had to double its production capacity?

29 Which sugar-free drink did Coca-Cola launch?

30 What were the average annual earnings at investment bank Goldman Sachs?

31 Which firm had to delay the launch of its PlayStation 3 in the UK?

32 Which company had to deal with an unexpected rush of orders following its TalkTalk 'free broadband' promotion?

33 Which chocolate manufacturer recalled over 1 million bars of chocolate?

34 Which country introduced a tax on chopsticks? Why?

35 Why were Warren Buffet and Richard Branson in the news?

36 Which two building societies announced a proposed merger?

37 What was the Cyclepod?

38 For which company did Ken Lay work? Why was this company famous?

39 Which rival to the Barbie doll underwent a revamp?

40 Why did over 1 million council workers go on strike?

41 What was the fastest-growing private limited company?

42 Which US state sued major car manufacturers for the environmental damage caused by their products?

43 Why were two directors of online betting companies arrested?

44 Which crisp manufacturer refused to allow Tesco to sell its products?

45 Which high-street retailer won the Business in the Community Award for Excellence?

46 Which was the fastest-growing technology company?

47 Which firm bought Pilkington Glass?

48 What is meant by the 'private equity boom'?

49 Which communications company wrote off over £20 billion of goodwill?

50 Who was nominated as the most powerful person in business by the *Sunday Times*?